REVISED EDITION

YOUR EMOTIONAL FITNESS

Everything you need to know
to live a life of Abundance

by Gary Rubin

BALBOA.
PRESS
A DIVISION OF HAY HOUSE

Balboa Press books may be ordered through booksellers or by contacting:

Balboa Press
A Division of Hay House
1663 Liberty Drive
Bloomington, IN 47403
www.balboapress.com
1-(877) 407-4847

Print information available on the last page.

ISBN: 978-1-4525-7059-4 (sc)
ISBN: 978-1-4525-7060-0 (e)
ISBN: 978-1-4525-7061-7 (hc)

Library of Congress Control Number: 2013904729

Balboa Press rev. date: 8/16/2016

This book is dedicated to everyone who read the original version of Your Emotional Fitness... and to my sister Shelley for the countless hours she spent helping with the editing and re-write of both this book and the original version... and, of course, to my daughter Jessica.

———

This revised edition was created because, after living the principles in the original version for over 3 years, my life was transformed to an even higher level. My desire is to update, abridge, revise, and enhance some of the information presented. It was an act of love to create this book. Thank you for allowing me to share it with you.

———

**"If you want to awaken all of humanity,
then awaken all of yourself.
If you want to eliminate all the
suffering in the world,
then eliminate all that is dark and negative
within yourself.
Truly, the greatest gift you have to give
is that of your own self transformation"**

—Lao Tzu

TABLE OF CONTENTS

1. INTRODUCTION

Many years ago I was working for a construction company. One day, while having lunch with some co-workers, a guy we called Foont said, *"Damn! Bologna sandwiches again! Every stinkin' day I get nothin' but bologna sandwiches. I hate bologna sandwiches!"* *"So,"* one of the other guys said, *"why don't you ask your wife to make you something else?"* *"Won't do any good"* he said. *"I make my own lunch."*

We have numerous choices every day, from things that are simple and routine to the more profound choices that impact our relationships, our careers, and our lives. These choices are generally based on our thoughts and beliefs about events in the world around us.

Every time you have a thought and choose to believe it, you initiate a biochemical reaction in your body which we call an emotion. This emotion will then illicit a response or reaction within you. How you react to your thoughts will impact your life experience.

Events are reality. And your resistance to reality is what can transform these events into personal problems. It is actually possible to never have another problem for the rest of your life. By dealing with events and the reality of the situation and not the blocked energy inside of you, you'll find there is nothing to deal with except your own fears and desires.

The light at the end of the tunnel is not an illusion...the tunnel is.

Is this the life you hoped to be living? Imagine living your life... feeling love and acceptance towards others and experiencing inner happiness no matter what is going on in the world outside of you. You can do this for yourself, if you choose. Actually, YOU are the only one who can make this happen. Go ahead, it's so easy to get started...just begin by turning the page...

"A journey of a thousand leagues begins with a single step."
—Confucius

1.1 MY GOAL FOR YOU

If you found a message in a bottle, and on the outside of the bottle it read "The message inside contains what you need most for a happy, fulfilled, and abundant life", what would the message written inside say?

The purpose of this book is to help you take control of your life and be able to create the life of abundance that you want and deserve. A definition of abundance that I relate to is: *a fullness of spirit which overflows, along with a lifestyle of more than adequate material provisions.* Take a moment to think about what your definition of abundance might be.

This is not a self-help book, but a self-empowerment book. Its purpose is to change your state of consciousness and your perceptions of life. If you choose to allow yourself to learn the powerful principles contained herein, the information in this book will guide you towards your emotional fitness.

> *"You are led through your lifetime by your inner learning creature,*
> *the playful spiritual being that is your real self."*
> —Richard Bach

If things in your life are not happening as you like, and you make an effort to fix the symptoms (the problems you're experiencing), you will only get a temporary solution. If you try to fix what is happening on the outside…bad job, unfulfilling relationships, challenging financial situation, ill health, etc…without changing how you interpret the situation from inside, you will need constant reminders and motivation to behave in the way you have decided would be best for you. But the moment you see and perceive things differently, change is natural and inevitable.

> *"When you change the way you look at things…*
> *the things you look at change."*
> —Wayne Dyer

It's not about cleaning the projection (what is on the outside), but cleaning the projector (you)...so you can let in more light. By cleaning the lens (your thoughts, perceptions, beliefs) and letting in more light, you create a shift of awareness, which gives you new perspectives...a new way of seeing and being in the world.

"Yesterday I was clever, so I wanted to change the world.
Today I am wise, so I am changing myself."
—Rumi

Everything in your life, perfect or not, is you. Because of this, you have the power to change it. Facing, learning from, and transforming negative feelings is a conscious choice which requires a commitment to release the negative emotions holding you back. Once you've released these negative feelings and thoughts, your health and happiness will take a turn for the better. You will no longer see your struggles as a tragedy, but instead an opportunity for your development into a more flexible human being. Your struggles actually become stepping stones to a better life.

You will learn to appreciate all of your emotions, even negative ones, because your negative emotions become a call to action, letting you know that something is amiss inside of you. Negative emotions are a signal that some kind of change is needed, and if you handle the negative emotions when they are small, the situation will not become a crisis. For example, instead of letting things escalate until you are infuriated, you will make the change when you begin to get annoyed. It is an empowering way to live! Furthermore, having transcended emotional pain, you'll have more compassion for others who are still lost in turmoil.

What you will find truly amazing is that when you start to see things differently and change your perceptions, the old problems on the outside miraculously resolve themselves and new opportunities just appear out of nowhere. It becomes the process of creation at its best. It's not a matter of what you are doing...it's all a matter of what you are being.

"I have invented the world I see."
—A Course in Miracles

You may even experience a feeling that something is missing from your life, and then realize that what is missing are the old problems and the stress. Now you see the things that happen as just life situations and opportunities, not problems.

> *"We cannot choose our external circumstances,*
> *but we can always choose how we respond to them."*
> —Epictetus

This book will give you a deeper understanding of the choices that you have, and help you become empowered to make the most important choice of all...the choice to choose your thoughts and beliefs. Once you realize that your beliefs create your thoughts and in turn your reality, you will be able to take control of your life.

Please remember that the process of self-empowerment is never ending and has no time frame, yet results can be seen immediately. As soon as you are no longer seeing a limiting picture of your potential, you can become aware that all is perfect...even if everything in your life has told you otherwise. You've been living that old way long enough. Isn't it time to allow for something new? You don't need to understand anything, you just need to allow...

> *"Trying to understand is like straining to see through muddy water.*
> *Be still, and allow the mud to settle.*
> *Remain still, until it is time to act."*
> —Lao Tzu

The principles within this book will change your state of consciousness and your perceptions of life. With the knowledge of "self" that you will gain, it is my hope that you will be empowered to take control and create the life of abundance that you so richly deserve.

> *"The world is missing what can be found in you."*
> —James Miller

1.2 ABOUT THIS BOOK

Within these pages is a compilation of all the valuable information I have acquired through many years of study and life experiences. These studies include training and practice in Life Coaching, Energy Leadership™, Neuro Linguistic Programming (NLP), and Hypnosis, as well as many other trainings and readings in the field of personal growth and psychology. What has motivated me to write this book is not what I learned, but how my life has been transformed by what I've learned. If this book helps you on the path towards your own transformation, I will have achieved my goal.

"No man can reveal to you aught but that which already lies half asleep in the dawning of your knowledge. The teacher gives not of his wisdom but rather of his faith and his lovingness. If he is indeed wise he does not bid you to enter the house of his wisdom, but rather leads you to the threshold of your own mind."
—Kahlil Gibran

After spending countless hours researching the fields of Personal Growth, Psychology, and Spiritual Psychology, I learned that there are two extremes. Success trainers like Tony Robbins will teach you about your *Unlimited Power* and how to *Awaken the Giant Within*. These types of trainers will help you to see how to access all of your personal power based on the philosophy of total self-creation. On the other end of the spectrum are teachers like the ancient philosopher Lao Tzu, who instructs on how to go with the flow and to live in the moment, allowing your life to unfold and trusting in the wisdom of the Universe.

Which way is better; using laser focus and intensity or going with the flow and allowing? That would be like asking *"Would you rather ride a bicycle that has a properly inflated front tire or back tire?"* For a smooth ride, you will want both tires balanced with the right amount of pressure.

If your focus is solely on achievement and accomplishing goals, you might find yourself unfulfilled yet living in luxury. You may long for the peace you see in others with far less.

If your focus is solely on allowing your life to unfold and trusting in the wisdom of the Universe, you may eventually yearn for the material comforts you see others enjoying, and might even resent the fact that the Universe has not provided for you sufficiently.

The key to a life of balance is to passionately pursue what you desire, and at the same time understand that your happiness is not dependent on achieving whatever it is you are seeking. When we take the pressure off of ourselves to produce results at any cost, and instead follow our inner wisdom and trust in the process of life, things often unfold better than we could have ever imagined.

The purpose of this book is to help you achieve that balance in your life…so you can have and enjoy all the things that money can buy, and also have and enjoy all the things that money cannot buy.

Whether we are happy or not depends on our inner harmony, not on other people or events. Certainly we should keep on learning how to master our outside circumstances, because our comfort and survival may well depend on it. But such mastery will not add one bit of joy to how we feel, or reduce the chaos of the world as we experience it. To do this, we must learn to achieve mastery over our own consciousness, state of being, and Emotional Fitness.

1.3 HOW YOU ARE WIRED

The first step on your path to emotional fitness is to understand how you, as a human being, are "wired."

Events in your life have no meaning until they reach the part of your brain called the limbic system, which is more commonly known as your unconscious mind. The unconscious mind asks *"What does this mean?"* as it is a human condition to try to make sense of things. The next step is very interesting. Within your unconscious mind a little voice that was formed in your childhood retrieves a memory from the past and connects it to what's going on now, thereby telling the unconscious a story about what the event means. The nervous system is convinced the interpretation is real and produces feelings. You will believe that your feelings are true, so if you are feeling bad from the understanding the little voice created, you will then react with an attitude...and then behaviors and actions. Other people are influenced by these actions and behaviors and they respond to you accordingly. After creating your reality, do you ever blame other people and situations for your world not working the way you wish it would?

The next thing that happens is this experience reinforces your self-image, which is what caused your initial interpretation. It all happens in the blink of an eye...and becomes an endless cycle...a snowball becomes an avalanche.

Moreover, when danger is perceived by the unconscious part of the brain, the body reacts with a "fight or flight" response. In fact, as the brain takes in negative information, it converts this information into chemicals (toxins), and it then lets your whole body know that there's trouble in your world. These toxins are stress hormones, and "injecting" bad news, real or imagined, has the same effect as injecting a chemical into your body. (More on this in the chapter *Poison or the Fountain of Youth...It's Your Choice.*)

This part of your emotional brain is left over from our prehistoric past, when people scavenged for food and needed to react quickly, for example, if a lion suddenly appeared and decided you were lunch. But in modern, complex human situations, this on/off switch can be triggered too easily, allowing us to see danger when a cool head would be a wiser and safer choice. To make matters worse, if you had a difficult childhood, you may be seeing danger everywhere in an attempt to keep yourself safe...but instead, it's making you miserable. Do you want to be miserable? Of course not, but you are unconsciously afraid that if you let your guard down, something terrible may sneak up on you while you're not paying attention.

During the first seven or eight years of life, the mind absorbs all information without question. It is during this time that the beliefs and values that will be with a person throughout his/her life are formed... beliefs about who they are and what the world represents to them, about success and failure, right and wrong, good and bad, love, money, charity, etc. The unconscious mind creates a particularly deep connection with beliefs caused by traumatic experiences, such as when we felt judged, criticized, or not accepted, because those are the beliefs that we think helped us survive or overcome our experience (more on this in the chapter *Parenting*).

If you are tired of being governed by your unconscious, and want to stop feeling as if hungry lions are jumping out at you when someone says the wrong thing, looks at you the wrong way, or cuts you off in traffic, here's the good news: in another part of your brain called the neo-cortex (your thinking brain), more commonly known as your conscious mind, you can question if you are really in danger. The challenge is that in a battle between the unconscious and the conscious, the unconscious will usually win. Think of your conscious mind as the captain of the ship and your unconscious mind as the crew. Even though the captain wants to believe he's in charge, an uncooperative crew will compromise the captain's control. Are you walking around in a state of mutiny? Do you know other people who are?

"Nothing is either good or bad. It's thinking that makes it so."
—William Shakespeare

Your brain is a wonderful instrument that awaits your every command. If you compare the thinking power of your brain to a computer, it would take the equivalent of over 5,000 miles of wiring to operate. Your brain contains about 28 billion neurons, which are nerve cells that conduct impulses and interpret the information you receive through your senses, and then convey that information to your brain. In fact, each one of these neurons is a self-contained computer capable of processing over one million bits of information. The power of your brain to process information is staggering. This enormous computer runs your heart, lungs, blood flow, and so much more, without you being consciously aware. In fact, your body is a universe in motion. You are 50 trillion cells working together in harmony. With all of this power, you may be asking yourself why you can't just shake off depression and frustrations and be happy and content all the time. Well, you can!

Your body is energy, pure and simple, and whether you are aware of it or not, you are constantly manipulating this energy. When you increase the positive energy, you become so much more alive.

"Everything is energy and that's all there is to it. Match the frequency of the reality that you want and you cannot help but get that reality. It can be no other way. This is not philosophy. This is physics."
—Albert Einstein

What if you, on a conscious level, could decide what things mean, instead of unconsciously allowing old fears to decide? What if you realized that you can change the meaning of any event or anything someone has said to you, and consequently change how you feel, the decisions you make, and, ultimately, your destiny? Would you then create a life that is happy, fulfilled, and abundant...no matter what was happening in the world around you? That's emotional fitness...and achieving that is my intent for you with this book.

"It's not what you look at that matters, it's what you see."
—Henry David Thoreau

2. YOUR EMOTIONAL FITNESS

Emotional fitness is so much more than positive thinking. Your thoughts have no power until you infuse them with your energy and consciousness, which comes from your perceptions and beliefs. It is these perceptions and beliefs that determine the quality of the energy that is emanating from you.

As an emotionally fit person, you will realize that the only meaning anything has is the meaning that you give it, and the interpretations you give the events in your life are what will determine your destiny. When you choose an empowering way of thinking about everything that happens, that will become your reality, because that will be the energy you are broadcasting. Ask yourself, *"Are my thoughts and words in harmony with the world I wish to create?"*

> *"If you are distressed by anything external, the pain is not due to the thing itself, but to your own estimate of it, and this you have the power to revoke at any moment."*
> —Marcus Aurelius

The amount of information that comes pouring in through our five senses is remarkable, but your unconscious mind is constantly deleting, distorting, and generalizing, so you are consciously left with only a tiny fraction of this information…and that is your reality. In other words, your internal representation of reality is a miniscule fraction of actual reality.

According to the book *What the Bleep Do We Know*, we are aware of 2,000 bits of information out of the 400 billion bits of information we are processing per second. Similarly, Mihaly Czikszentmihalyi, in his book *Flow: The Psychology of Optimal Performance*, explains that of the approximately 2 million bits of information that you process per second, you are aware of only 156 bits. The reason that these numbers vary is because no one has determined how much a "bit" is. But what has been determined is the colossal difference in what we are conscious of compared to what is really happening. For simplicity, let's just use round numbers and say that our conscious awareness retains approximately 200 bits of the 2 million that we are processing unconsciously, or 1/100th of one percent.

The way you think is what determines which bits of information you internalize out of all the information that is available. So it's more about changing the way you think than about changing your thoughts, because it is the way you think that creates your thoughts and determines your interpretation of events. Your thought processes are based on your internal perceptions, and your internal perceptions usually stem from your past experiences. You need to consciously realize that your thoughts have a hand in all your experiences, or you'll go through life asking *"why is this happening to me?"*

Positive and negative thinking is generated in the conscious mind, our thinking mind. It is our conscious mind that solves problems and creates dreams, aspirations, and desires. In contrast, our unconscious mind is where all of our habits and learned behaviors are stored. When you find yourself having an unwanted reaction to a thought or an event, it's old programming from your unconscious mind.

Have you ever made the conscious decision to stop doing some unwanted behavior…or thinking some unwanted thought…yet found yourself still doing it? Simply thinking positive thoughts on a conscious level will not change thoughts and behaviors that are generated on an unconscious level.

"Positive thinking will not help you do anything better.
However, it will help you do everything better than negative thinking will."
—Zig Ziglar

Engaging in negative thinking is unhealthy because it makes things seem worse than they are. Negative thoughts can have a snowball effect. For example, an event can trigger a negative thought which can lead to a mild case of the blues. This one negative thought usually leads to another, and then another, which may eventually lead to a distorted perception of reality. Negative thoughts can lead to negative emotions, and we tend to believe that our emotions reflect the truth. But if the thought leading to the emotion is not rational, "trusting your feelings" is a risky thing to do. Depression can be caused by falling into this cycle of negative thinking and forgetting the original trigger. Negative thoughts are not a symptom of depression, they are the cause of it. However, it is important not to energize negative thoughts as something to be avoided, rather just accept the negative thought as something you do not want …and allow it to fade away.

> *"Those thoughts that receive our attention, good or bad, go into the unconscious to become the fuel for later events in the real world."*
> —James Allen

Next time you're in a bad mood, remember that your day does not create your mood, your mood creates your day. Every emotion that you experience is because of a thought, not because of a person or thing that is influencing you.

> *"What is the key to releasing yourself from emotional prison? Simply this: Your thoughts create your emotions; therefore, your emotions cannot prove that your thoughts are accurate. Unpleasant feelings merely indicate that you are thinking something negative and believing it. Your emotions follow your thoughts just as surely as baby ducks follow their mother. But the fact that the baby ducks follow faithfully along doesn't prove that the mother knows where she is going."*
> —David D. Burns

Just like a thermostat operates by keeping the temperature within a predefined range, the unconscious mind is constantly operating in the background to keep us within our predefined settings. There may be temporary changes, but more often than not, things return to how they were. You can change this by understanding how your unconscious mind works and by changing your approach. In order to create real change you need to "reset" your unconscious settings. (Your unconscious mind is discussed at length in Chapter 4, Your Unconscious Mind)

> *"We should not pretend to understand the world only by the intellect. The judgment of the intellect is only part of the truth."*
> —Carl Jung

Become the awareness behind your mind. Sometimes we are so caught up in our thoughts and emotions that it seems like we are in a raging river and all we see are the turbulent waters around us. Becoming the awareness would be like getting up on a bridge above the wild and violent river, where we can look down calmly and have an understanding of what is happening, as opposed to drowning in the quickly moving currents of thought and emotion.

Do you realize that your choices, either consciously or unconsciously, have played a part in the person you have become? Every skill you learn creates a new neural pathway and every thought you think creates a unique pattern in your brain. All changes in your mood are conveyed to every part of your body, altering the chemical activity. Your choices, which are a result of your core energy, have produced the thoughts, feelings and actions that have created the person you are today. By changing your core energy, you will get different results…a different you (we will discuss your core energy at length in the chapter *Your Energy*).

> *"If you cannot accept that you are co-creating all of the conditions,*
> *circumstances, and events of your life, at least accept that you*
> *are creating your experience of them. No one else can tell you*
> *how to feel about anything. Surely that is undeniable."*
> —Neale Donald Walsch

Everything happens for a reason. If you find that the reason does not serve you, ask yourself for the reason again…until you find a reason that empowers you. No matter how big your problems are, there have been people who have overcome far worse with ease and grace, and who may have even had some fun in the process, by choosing perceptions which best served them. And that, my friend, is emotional fitness.

> *"There is a story of a woman running away from tigers. She runs and runs*
> *and the tigers are getting closer and closer. When she comes to the edge of*
> *a cliff, she sees some vines there, so she climbs down and hangs on to the*
> *vines. Looking down, she sees that there are tigers below her as well. She*
> *then notices that a mouse is gnawing away at the vines. She also sees a*
> *beautiful bunch of strawberries close by, growing out of a clump of grass.*
> *She looks up and she looks down. She looks at the mouse. Then she just*
> *takes a strawberry, puts it in her mouth, and enjoys it thoroughly."*
> —Pema Chodron (from the Wisdom of No Escape)

2.1 STRESS

The purpose of this chapter is to help you to minimize or eliminate stress. Without getting rid of the stresses accumulated during your lifetime and learning how to avoid stress in the future, it will be very difficult for you to have the happiness and peace of mind you desire.

Stress is harmful to you because when danger, *either real or imagined*, is perceived by the unconscious part of the brain, the body reacts with a "fight or flight" response. You react to this negative information, suffer from the toxins that it creates, and end up with dis-stress and dis-ease. In fact, the World Health Association estimates that 80% of all illnesses are directly or indirectly caused by stress.

Imagine the world without humans. The stars, the moon, the plants, the animals, everything…and you'll see that it is all perfect, just the way it is. Without humans, nothing needs to be justified or judged, it is all just fine. Now, add humans to the equation, but without the ability to judge, and you will find that we are as perfect as the rest of creation. We are not good or bad, right or wrong. We are just the way we are, like the rest of nature.

Therefore, to avoid the stresses of day to day living, you simply need to eliminate judgment. I do not mean having good judgment or bad judgment; I mean constantly evaluating, labeling, analyzing, classifying, and rating. I know it's hard to give up judgment. You may never completely get rid of it. However, every effort you make will increase your chances of moving forward on a great path.

Remember the story of The Garden of Eden? Adam and Eve had to leave paradise when they ate from the tree of the knowledge of good and evil. When has judging something as good or evil taken you away from paradise?

> "Out beyond ideas of wrong doing and right doing, there is a field.
> I'll meet you there."
> —Rumi

The next thing you need to do to rid your life of stress is to give up the need to know why things happened the way they did. If you are putting your energy into the pain of your past, you are honoring this pain to a greater degree than you are honoring your present and future, thereby allowing this unfinished business to rob you of a happy and vibrant life right now. Until you can release the past and all the baggage that comes with it, you will not be able to move forward.

I had a client who spent 40 years in pain because of something that was said in five minutes. I asked her to consider which was worse... what was said to her in the past or what she was continually doing to herself. The next step was for her to put the 40 years and the five minutes into perspective. We used an NLP technique where she saw the old event, in black and white, in front of her face, and then moved it farther and farther away until it was the size of a speck. Then she envisioned all that she was grateful for in her life...and she moved this picture closer and closer until it was bright and in living color right in front of her face. She then felt the emotion of how this made her feel. She felt better because she had simply changed her internal representation and put everything into perspective. Since we don't live in black and white, visualizing a memory in black and white will lessen its grip on you. And when you make the picture small, you stop "blowing things out of proportion."

> *"People become attached to their burdens*
> *sometimes more than the burdens are attached to them."*
> —George Bernard Shaw

When you get really good at recognizing your internal images, you can stop in the middle of a strong reaction and look and listen to what is going on in your mind. These internal pictures, sounds, and feelings are signals from your unconscious. If the signal is a voice in your head that does not serve you, turn down the volume...way down. If it's a picture, push it far away, so it becomes small and dim. If it's a feeling, make it small and soft, then let it leave your body and become a memory of a feeling you used to experience.

Another example of the way our internal pictures work is revealed in this next story. I was speaking with a client who was extremely stressed over an impending business deal. He had done all he could, and was awaiting the results. I asked him what it was like. He first tried to tell me about the problem, and I said I didn't want an explanation of his situation, as that was the story he was telling over and over again, strengthening its grip on him. He then started to tell me his emotional responses to the problem, and I said I only wanted to know what it was like. As he went on to tell me the consequences of his reaction to the problem, I said "no, what is it like?" Frustrated, he said it was like he was on a raft in churning water, with darkness all around him, and a dark and looming sky. I asked him to look around and tell me what else he saw. Off to the right he saw mild rapids in the water, where the water was running over some rounded rocks down to a pool of calm serene water. Beyond this pool of calm water was a beautiful sky and horizon…a wonderful scene. I then asked him what he was doing about this situation, and he said he was paddling furiously, trying to get to the calm water. *"How is that working for you"* I asked. *"It isn't"* he said. So I asked him what might work better. I saw a sense of calm come over him as he said he should just relax in the raft, and allow the currents to take him where he needed to go, as it was time to put down the paddle and trust in the process.

You don't have to just accept how you are feeling or thinking, you can dig down and witness the creation of that feeling; what are the images, sounds or internal dialogue, and where in your body do you experience the feeling? What happens if you change something? This internal dialogue happens in the blink of an eye, and is so simple to change. We are creating it all the time unconsciously…isn't it time to easily change to a conscious decision?

By altering the images, sounds and feelings inside, we can heal from traumatic experiences, increase our problem solving ability, and become more adept at dealing with a wider range of situations. Allow yourself to change the way you think about thinking…and make better choices about how to function. If you tell me you feel a certain way, I will not ask you why…I will ask you how? If I ask you why, you will tell me the same story that you have been rehearsing for most of your life, proving the validity of your feelings. But if you tell me how, then it becomes easy for you to change HOW you feel. If I ask you how you do depressed, and how you do happy, it becomes clear that you can choose either path. Which one will you choose right now?

> *"The greatest weapon against stress is our ability*
> *to choose one thought over another."*
> —William James

Consider times in the past when you may have let something trivial affect your day, such as a slow person in line, an aggressive driver, or anyone

16

else behaving in a way of which you do not approve. None of us really know if something is good or bad. A perceived frustration may actually end up being a "blessing in disguise."

Try this: Get out of your own way and allow your life to unfold in a way that may be perfect, but doesn't look that way from your present point of view. Make a conscious decision to give up judgment and the need to know why things are happening the way they are.

"Today I shall judge nothing that occurs.
Non judgment creates a silence in my mind."
—A Course in Miracles

When stress enters your life, realize that you have four choices... avoid it, accept it, change it, or change your perspective of it. My interactions with my teenage daughter were once very stressful. This stress was actually not from her, but from my interpretations of her actions. I was judging her attitude as being rude and disrespectful. Then, I realized that I could not avoid her attitude, I didn't want to accept it, I certainly couldn't change it, as I had been trying that for years, so I decided to change my interpretation. I now interpret her attitude as an outlet for the pain that comes with being a teenager. Instead of getting angry, I feel compassion. Consequently, instead of being out of control, I am very much in control. And an amazing thing resulted... her attitude got better. I learned that you cannot fight darkness by bringing in more darkness, only by bringing in the light. Being stressed only adds to darkness.

"Know that darkness is merely the absence of light.
You can be the small candle that defeats the vast darkness."
—Jonathan Lockwood Huie

That which you resist will persist...so I stopped resisting, because to do so is simply putting energy towards that which I cannot control.

"Resistance is thought transformed into feeling.
Change the thought that creates the resistance, and there is no more resistance."
—Robert Conklin

Have you ever been on an airplane that hit some bad turbulence? Did you choose stress or to enjoy the ride? If you chose stress, did you make up a movie in your mind about the horrible plane crash that was about to occur? Since you are here with me now, I guess there was no plane crash. Problem is…your body did not know that you were just fantasizing. Your body reacted as if the movie in your mind was real. In a later chapter, *Poison or the Fountain of Youth…It's Your Choice*, you will learn about all of the harm this type of thought creates. Next time you experience turbulence, I hope you will decide to enjoy the ride. Since you cannot avoid it or change it, you may as well accept it and change your perspective. If the plane is going to crash, try to find a clump of strawberries to enjoy, just as the lady hanging from the vines did in the previous chapter.

"Ultimately, nothing matters very much.
The defeat that seems to break your heart today will be nothing but a ripple among the waves of other experiences in the ocean of your life further ahead."
—Napoleon Hill

2.2 YOUR ENERGY

It is not a question of *whether* you can create what happens in your life…
you already are creating your reality, right now! Life is about aligning your
energy, both consciously and unconsciously, so that it naturally attracts
positive realities. You are not your mind, you are not your body, you are
not your emotions…you are so much more…you are energy.

> *"The energy of the mind is the essence of life."*
> —Aristotle

The goal here is to get you to think about, and be aware of, your
energy levels and those of people around you.

According to the Core Energy Coaching™ Process, your core energy
is the energy you are generating from your core beliefs, which reside in
your unconscious mind. For example, if your core energy is that of a
victim, all of your behaviors and actions will be in harmony with that
energy. If your core energy is anger, all actions and behaviors will be
congruent with rage. Even if you are able to consciously control your
negative energy…as soon as you are under stress, your unconscious will
override and your core negative energy will take over…because this energy
is your unconscious programming. If your core energy is peace, you will
have serenity regardless of what is happening in your life situation.

> *"Peace, as the world commonly understands it, comes when the*
> *summer sky is clear and the sun shines in scintillating beauty, when the*
> *pocketbook is full and the mind and body are free of ache and pain…*
> *but…true peace…is a calmness of the soul amid terrors of trouble,*
> *inner tranquility amid the howl and rage of the outer storm."*
> —Martin Luther King

Core Energy leads to thought…thought leads to emotion…emotion
leads to action…which sometimes results in a statement like "Why did I
do that?" or "I wish that hadn't happened". This statement then reinforces
the original thought and feeling. For example, let's say you are skiing and

you approach the top of an advanced run. You think, "Wow, this is steep" which results in an emotion...fear...and because of the fear, your focus is on not falling. However, because your unconscious doesn't see negatives, your focus becomes the action of falling. Chances are you will fall, which will reinforce your original belief and result in a thought such as "I knew that run was too steep." It all began with the thought... well, actually, it began with your core energy (which was inadequacy), which then created the thought.

What would have happened if your core energy was that of reconciliation (which contains a lot less fear then inadequacy), where things were not judged as good or bad? At the top of the slope, you would have asked the question "How can I do this?" That question would have resulted in a feeling of confidence and your brain would have answered (your brain will always answer the questions you ask it) by showing you how to go from one spot to the next, all the way down the hill, resulting in a thought like "I knew I could do that." By taking charge of your energy, you create the thought which creates the emotion, which creates the world in which you live.

"The Universe is constantly saying yes to us. It only says yes.
It is our task to discover what within us it is saying yes to."
—Lenedra J Carrol

When people try to change their behavior and old habits, it is a lot easier when core energy is in alignment with outer actions. Have you ever remained calm while you were angry inside? Didn't the anger just eat away at you? Did you live with that anger for a long time? Are you still mad at that horrible person who did that dastardly deed? If your core energy is anger, but you try to react differently (without anger), it may seem to be a good idea, but you will still be stressed and will release harmful chemicals into your body. A smart choice is instead to change your energy level to a more anabolic (constructive, building) energy level. If you get mad at other drivers, change your interpretation of that other driver. The action of cutting you off or driving too slow has nothing to do with you. All the rude people, mean people, etc...they are not being that way because of you. So wouldn't it be a wiser choice to not feel like a victim?

The table below shows some possible core energy levels and the thoughts and feelings associated with them. They are ordered by the lowest level (Victim) to the highest level (Non-Judgment). This table is derived from the Energetic Self Perception Chart which was developed by Bruce D Schneider, founder of the Institute for Professional Excellence in Coaching (iPEC), and author of the bestselling book, *Energy Leadership* (where you can find the original chart).

Energy Level[a]	Emotion	Action/ Result	Life View	Winning/ Losing
1. Victim	Apathy	Lethargy	I hate myself	I lose
2. Conflict	Anger	Defiance	I hate you	You lose
3.Responsibility	Forgiveness	Cooperation	I forgive you	I win
4. Concern	Compassion	Service	I feel for you	You win
5.Reconciliation	Peace	Acceptance	I understand you	We both win
6. Synthesis	Joy	Wisdom	I am you	Everyone always wins
7. Non-Judgment	Absolute passion	Creation	I am	Winning/ losing are illusions
Information on Energy Leadership is protected by copyright and used with permission of Bruce D Schneider and the Institute for Professional Excellence in Coaching. This material may not be reproduced or distributed in any format.				

The two lowest energy levels are described in detail in the chapters that follow (chapter 2.3 Understanding Anger and chapter 2.4 Overcoming Victim and Conflict (Anger) Energy). According to Schneider's model, Level 1 and Level 2 energies are catabolic (draining, destructive energies). When experienced on a long-term basis, catabolic energies cause pain and illness.

Level 1, Victim energy is the lowest level of energy and is indicative of thoughts, beliefs, emotions and perceptions that result in feelings of powerlessness. This level of energy may cause you to "put your head in the sand"…to hide from, avoid, or live at the effect of what is happening around you. Are there any situations in your life where you are "putting your head in the sand" or where you just "don't feel like" moving forward?

Level 2, Conflict energy is the predominant energy that we experience in the world around us. This energy includes anger, struggle, defiance, and antagonism. It is the feeling that others must lose so that you can win, which at times may be the case…but there are usually more

21

powerful, healthier ways to achieve winning results. This level can also be where the feelings of victim energy manifest themselves into action and become anger. Frequently, energy will cycle between victim and anger; unused energy from the victim level will accumulate, build up and ultimately be expressed as anger. When the energy from anger is expended, the energy level then returns to the lower victim level. The result is a continuous "unhappy cycle" of anger to apathy and back again.

There is a reason many people unconsciously choose to engage at lower energy levels. When you are at level 1, in a state of victim energy, you have an excuse for avoiding obligations. Victim energy may also bring sympathy, reduce guilt (not my fault), create a way of punishing others, justify addictions, and even create a way to dominate others. Existing at level 2's conflict energy, you might accomplish tasks by yourself, and/or can motivate others through aggression, fear, and force.

We all experience level 1 and 2 energy at times, which is perfectly normal. Bear in mind, though, according to Schneider, *normal* does not mean *required*. You can make the conscious choice at any time to choose the most appropriate energy level for you.

The next five levels of Schneider's model are anabolic (constructive, building) energies which produce healing of the body and the mind. We will go into greater depth on the subject of catabolic energy versus anabolic energy in the chapter *Poison or the Fountain of Youth...it's your choice.*

Level 3, Responsibility, is the start of anabolic energy. At this level, people begin to take responsibility for their thoughts, emotions, and actions, and realize that the content of their thoughts is up to them. The focus is winning, and hoping the other person can win too, but concentrating most on securing individual success. People at this level are masters at rationalization, as rationalizing is a great path out of the two lower levels. Living at the level of responsibility, it is natural to help yourself and others find ways to cope, release, and forgive. This level also provides tools to explain away resentment, stress, and other burdens.

Level 4, Concern introduces a feeling of compassion towards others, and a desire to be of service. At this level, people can reason objectively without taking things personally. A person living at concern will feel that a true win for them is when the other person wins first, because the need to be of service supersedes the desire to do for themselves.

Level 5, Reconciliation is the energy found in the greatest leaders in all walks of life; people at this level see everything as an opportunity. The core thought is on reconciling and accepting differences rather than identifying and focusing on ways to change them. The primary belief at this level is a true win/win mentality. Inhabitants of lower levels give lip service to the concept of win/win, but this altitude embodies a walk the talk. Individuals at reconciliation are calm, powerful, and confident; feel an inner peace and contentment... and believe they are in control and can choose their life experience.

Level 6, Synthesis is the blending away of the belief that we are all separate. Masters of this level see everyone and everything as part of themselves, and themselves as part of everything else. It is at this altitude where intuition comes alive. Creative people tap into this energy to create new and exciting innovations for everyone's benefit. With the sense of connection, people at this level feel that everyone always wins, and that everything that happens has purpose and value. At synthesis, one feels a sense of pleasure, satisfaction, and joy.

Level 7, Non-Judgment is characterized by completely objective thinking and lack of fear. Commanders of this level believe that winning and losing are illusions; these are simply terms that people create for a game that is also self-created. No human can resonate completely at this elevation, but people can learn to access it. It is a state of oneness and being-ness...being one with God, one with the Universe or one with your higher self. We can be transported to this space through some spiritual practices and meditation, and some people can get there simply by being in nature.

Please realize that there are advantages and disadvantages at each level, and no one stays at any one location. Your energy will fluctuate throughout the day and amid your experiences. It is through conscious awareness that you choose which energy is most appropriate for your current situation. The Energy Leadership Index™ Assessment is an online survey that provides a profile of how your energy is distributed over the seven levels. Taking the assessment and being debriefed by an Energy Leadership Index Master Practitioner gains a greater understanding of how and why you operate the way you do, and gives you strategies for shifting to the energy levels you desire.

One way you can move to a higher level of consciousness (which means increasing your anabolic energy) is simply choosing which thoughts to recognize as "just a thought" versus those for which you will claim ownership. Do not make negative thoughts real by getting on the train of that thought, where your mind begins to associate one negative thought with another. You can instead decide the negative thought is something you do not want and allow it to fade away. Then choose a quality thought and hop on that train, arriving at a superior energy level. Remember: It is not the thoughts that come and go that make a difference, but the thoughts over which you take ownership and ponder throughout the day.

That the birds of worry and care fly over your head, this you cannot change, but that they build nests in your hair, this you can prevent."
—Chinese Proverb

Sometimes catabolic energy can serve as a call to action; a call for you to change your perceptions of your immediate environment, or to adjust an old belief that you have internalized. Schneider teaches that lowering your levels of victim and conflict energy will naturally increase your higher levels of energy. Even small amounts of catabolic energy will greatly affect your existing energetic makeup. This energetic makeup encompasses every thought, feeling, and emotion you have had today, every thought, feeling, and emotion you have ever experienced, and every action you have ever taken. These thoughts, feelings, and emotions are etched inside of you like data imprinted on a computer chip. One of the goals of this book is to help you recognize and overwrite the existing data that does not serve you, so you can live a life of your choosing, a life of abundance.

I think this quote from R.K. Ebert, the former director of Clinical Neuropsychological Services at Temple University Hospital says it all:

"Unmolested, our energy system maintains the body in a condition of maximal health and wellbeing. Disturbances in this system are brought about by repeated insults-waves of catabolic energy generated by consciousness. Healing involves shifting the energy generated in the conscious and unconscious processes. This is most efficiently accomplished by neutralizing the energy of "low level" thoughts, by disrupting the catabolic pattern of thought energy. There are no idle thoughts. All thoughts have an energetic consequence.. All thoughts create in their own likeness. Catabolic energy injures, anabolic energy heals."

2.3 UNDERSTANDING ANGER

Anger is the most common expression of catabolic energy (victim and conflict energy). This chapter is devoted to giving you an understanding of anger. The next chapter will give you ways to overcome victim and anger energy.

Do you know why people get angry? There are several reasons, but here are a few. If someone makes you feel inadequate, you will strike out in anger. If something you value is being threatened, you will feel anger. If someone is in emotional pain, they will be angry, and you will probably know they are angry by their behavior and the energy they exude. What they are really saying is "I am in pain, here is some for you".

> *"Anger is never without a reason, but seldom with a good one."*
> —Benjamin Franklin

We get angry because things are not happening the way we want, yet getting angry is the least effective way to achieve our desired outcome, because we are in our reactive (unconscious) mind instead of our thinking (conscious) mind. We are thinking, unconsciously, that if we get mad enough, the situation will change. Logically, when something goes wrong, wouldn't it be easier to just accept the situation and do what needs to be done? Instead, we create anger and unhappiness because we are attached to the idea it shouldn't have happened. You unconsciously believe that your anger gives you power, because it makes you right and the situation wrong. You unconsciously use your anger as a currency... thinking it can buy you a different outcome. Becoming aware that your anger will not have a positive effect on the outcome allows you to accept what is happening, which weakens and changes these feelings of anger.

> *"You will not be punished for your anger;*
> *you will be punished by your anger."*
> —Buddha

What about a rainy day? Do you ever get mad at the weather? Do you think if you get mad enough it will stop raining?

I still get angry when I see people talking on their cell phones while driving because it puts me and everyone else around them in danger. I then joke that if I get mad enough, they'll stop doing it. But wait...if I get mad enough, guess what? They'll keep talking on their cell phones while driving, and I'll compromise my good health and positive outlook by getting mad. I may even lessen my own concentration on the road and risk a calamity.

Perhaps it would be better to just accept things as they are, and make more rules for myself and less for others. If I don't want to accept things as they are, my only choices are to change them if I can, or to change my perception of them. Thanks...I feel better already.

"Energy cannot be created or destroyed,
it can only be changed from one form to another."
—Albert Einstein

Some kinds of anger can be positive. Anger motivated by compassion can be a powerful force to bring about swift and decisive action. Many leaders throughout our history were motivated by their anger to disrupt the status quo, and consequently made some powerful and profound changes. I am not talking about out of control anger, but anger energy focused on making a positive change. For example, you may get angry about starving children, which may motivate you to do something to help.

"The question is not whether we will be extremists, but what kind of
extremists we will be. Will we be extremists for hate or love? Will we be
extremists for the preservation of injustice or for the extension of justice."
—Martin Luther King

But anger, when not motivated by compassion, can lead to hatred... and hatred has no positive qualities at all. Destructive effects of hatred are easily visible. Feeling hatred entirely overwhelms a person, and destroys their peace and presence of mind; the very essence of their being.

"When we hate our enemies, we are giving them power over us; power
over our sleep, our appetites, our blood pressure, our health, and our
happiness. Our enemies would dance with joy if only they knew how

they were worrying us! Our hate is not hurting them at all, but our hate is turning our own days and nights into a hellish turmoil".
—Dale Carnegie

"Holding on to anger is like grasping a hot coal with the intent of throwing it at someone else; you are the one who gets burned."
—Buddha

The only cure for anger and hatred is to develop patience, tolerance, and compassion by being aware of your core energy and your perceptions. Which 200 bits of information out of the 200 million available are grabbing your attention? What additional information would you need to be aware of to change your perceptions? When you take a strong stance from a place of compassion and tolerance instead of anger and hate, everything becomes easy, because you have access to all of your intelligence and reasoning ability. When you never fall under the spell of anger, you will always have control of your world. Try this: When you get angry at someone or feel hatred towards another human being…realize that if you could take a look into their secret past, you would see enough pain and suffering to disarm all of your hostility, and then choose compassion instead.

"The first drawback of anger is that it destroys your inner peace; the second is that it distorts your view of reality. If you think about this and come to understand that anger is really unhelpful, that it is only destructive, you can begin to distance yourself from anger."
—Dalai Lama

Now…think about the people or events that give rise to your anger… and decide how you can change your perception and interpretation to one of understanding, tolerance, compassion, and love. Watch as your energy changes from negative to positive. Then, you decide which one feels better.

2.4 OVERCOMING VICTIM AND CONFLICT (ANGER) ENERGY

In order to obtain a high level energy, you need to overcome victim and anger energy. If you are currently operating at these lower energy levels, do not feel discouraged, 85% of the population is right there with you. Accomplishing an understanding of your perceptions and interpretations allows you to consciously choose the energy level that best serves you in each situation.

You will feel like a victim or become angry when you believe that your life experience is created outside of you...by other people and situations. *As soon as you take responsibility for creating your reality from the inside, you are no longer a victim, but the creator of your life.*

Sometimes being angry helps us overcome feelings of helplessness. This often appears as the need to be right. Prior to becoming enlightened, I was on a bike ride and a runner who was not paying attention was running towards us. He looked up, startled and shouted "SLOW DOWN". He obviously felt weakened by being startled, so he needed to make it our fault. Not to be out done, I shouted back "WATCH WHERE YOU'RE GOING YOU JERK". Immediately after shouting at him, I felt superior and powerful...I was right. Upon reflection, however, it is easy to see what really happened. He felt inferior so he needed to attack. Then, to overcome my victim energy, I attacked back (a little louder and more aggressive than him). This is how wars are started, friendships ruined, jobs lost. When we give up the need to be "right" and consciously become understanding and compassionate towards other people and situations, we are taking control of our thoughts...thus taking control of our consequences. The compulsion to be right usually stems from the emergence of ego and insecurities casting a shadow over an otherwise peaceful encounter.

> *"Where there is no accusation of 'fault', there can be no anger."*
> —Jonathan Lockwood Huie

Victor Frankl, an Austrian Psychotherapist and Nazi concentration camp survivor, drew on his brutal experiences to write *Man's Search for Meaning*, which includes the following ultimate truth...

> *"Everything can be taken from a man but one thing,*
> *the last of the human freedoms... to choose one's attitude to*
> *any given set of circumstances, to choose one's way."*
> —Victor Frankl

According to the Institute of Heartmath, five minutes of anger will suppress your immune system for six hours, and five minutes of love will strengthen your immune system for the same time period. In a later chapter, *Poison or the Fountain of Youth...it's your choice*, we will explore at length how anger affects your health.

Whatever happens to you, from little disappointments to heartbreaking grief, you get to decide how to feel about it...or more precisely...what it means. When you decide what it means, you will be deciding your reaction to it, and the resulting and corresponding level of happiness and joy in your life.

Whenever you are angry and ready to lose your temper, try to slow down, refrain from reacting, and just pause and take a deep breath.

Next, complete this exercise to center and gain control of yourself: As you inhale slowly, visualize healing white light coming into your body through your feet, and going through every cell of your body, nourishing each cell, all the way to your head, until the healing white light escapes from the top of your skull. Picture this flow of energy in the time it takes to breathe a long and slow inhale. Then, as you exhale, allow the healing white light to re-enter through the top of your head, filling and nourishing every cell in your body, until escaping out of the bottoms of your feet at the end of the exhale. A few or several breaths like this will work wonders for you. This simple exercise can be done anywhere, in the time it takes to take a long slow inhale and exhale.

Try it now...take a deep breath and think of everything for which you are grateful, and hold in your heart a feeling of gratitude. Feel this white light of gratitude as it bathes every cell of your body. The great thing about doing this gratitude exercise for a few minutes is you will begin to truly feel grateful for all the abundance in your life. If you are upset about something when you perform this exercise, your body will focus on the emotion that is most powerful, so make sure to feel the gratitude intensely.

"Gratitude unlocks the fullness of life. It turns what we have into enough and more. It turns denial into acceptance, chaos to order, confusion to clarity. It can turn a meal into a feast, a house into a home, a stranger into a friend. Gratitude makes sense of our past, brings peace for today, and creates a vision for tomorrow."
—Melody Beattie

Imagine you are driving in your car and finding yourself irritated. Start the white light exercise of calm bathing your body. You have to breathe anyway, so you may as well maximize the benefits.

Taking a test? Change the white light to one of intelligence, recall, or whatever skill you feel would be beneficial. Going into a stressful situation? Use the white light of confidence. Feeling insecure? Enjoy the white light of worthiness and confidence as it bathes each and every cell of your body.

A central theme of this book is the creation of neuro pathways, which are behaviors, beliefs, motivations, strategies, etc. within the unconscious mind and nervous system. Neuro pathways will be covered extensively in the chapter *Training your Mind*. The above centering exercise is one way to create a new neuro pathway in your mind, so that positive emotions become a natural and automatic event for you.

"Just close your eyes. Breathe. Stop whatever you're doing for ten seconds and find The Silence. Visit The Quiet. Just for ten seconds. Do it six times today. One minute a day. That's all it takes. One minute, divided into six parts. Go ahead. Do it now."
—Neale Donald Walsch

2.5 CONDITIONED BELIEFS

We spoke about conditioned beliefs or belief systems earlier; beliefs which were ingrained in you that you believed to be true. Beliefs can arise through verbal programming, or what you hear... modeling, what you see... or specific incidents, what you experience.

Your beliefs become unquestioned commands to your nervous system. They have the power to create and the power to destroy. Regardless of where our beliefs come from, we accept them as real and rarely question them. Some beliefs can be incredibly positive. For instance, an empowering belief can propel a person to great heights of abundance.

Unfortunately, people often develop limiting beliefs about who they are and of what they are capable. They believe that a failure to accomplish something in the past dictates a repeat failure if they try again. They say "why bother?" or "let's be realistic"...because they are living in fear of failure. Optimists are generally overachievers; they see failure as an event, not a person. When a pessimist fails, they believe they are a failure.

"A pessimist sees the difficulty in every opportunity.
An optimist sees the opportunity in every difficulty."
—Winston Churchill

Imagine a baby learning to walk, becoming unbalanced, and falling. After falling a dozen times, the parents decide that the baby is just not cut out for walking. Sounds ridiculous, but at some time in our lives we forget that falling is learning, and we decide not to try because we are afraid we might fall.

"When you curse yourself for falling down, you may be
cursing the very thing you needed to get to the next step."
—Dr. Mathew James

I know a lot of people who believe "you have to work hard to get ahead". I would like to tell you about a man named Hamdi, who owns and operates a restaurant in La Jolla, California called Berninis. I trust you

31

would agree that running a restaurant is a tough business and you have to work hard to be successful, but Hamdi makes it look easy. He never appears to be working, yet his business runs with precision. Why do some operators run around madly, yet he coasts along with effortless ease? It begins with his core energy, which results in his mental attitude. He believes it is easy, and so it is.

> *"Success is the ability to fulfill your desires with effortless ease."*
> —Deepak Chopra

"A bird in the hand is worth two in the bush". What a limiting belief that could be...if it kept you from taking actions that could effect a change in your life for the better. "Better the devil you know than the devil you don't know" creates a limitation in the same way.

"People don't change." If you are saying this about others, you may believe it about yourself. "You can't change bad habits". "That's just the way I am". Or maybe you believe that "old habits die hard" so you think it will be difficult for you to have emotional fitness after all these years. No...as a conscious adult...the way you are is the way you have chosen, and emotional fitness is always an attainable goal.

What about the conditioned beliefs that we pile upon ourselves because we expect the past to repeat itself? "I was hurt once, so I cannot trust anyone again." "I was unloved as a child, so I am not worthy of love." "The criticism I received as a child proves that I am not good enough." "I am poor, and destined to remain poor." "He or she doesn't love me, so I must be unworthy and will never find love."

Now think of some beliefs of your own. Can you question them and decide if you want to continue believing them? Do you know where your beliefs have come from? Did you make rules that govern your life... that you may want to change now that you are conscious of their origin?

Try this: Release the past and let go of your unfounded fears. Unchain the beliefs that do not serve you...and be careful to not suggest any fears or limiting beliefs to anyone, especially children.

> *"The real mission in life is to make yourself happy,*
> *and in order to be happy, you have to look at what you*
> *believe, the way you judge yourself, the way you*
> *victimize yourself."*
> —Don Miguel Ruiz – The Mastery of Love

Once we accept the perceptions of others as truth, their truths program into our unconscious as our truth. The problem is our unconscious does not reason, it just accepts the "program" without judgment, leading us to habitually engage in limiting and even inappropriate behaviors. Although most of our "programming" happened in childhood, we accept new programming whenever we decide to believe something. With repeated exposure to the "program" we form a new neuro pathway in our unconscious. This holds true for positive programming as well as negative programming. By becoming conscious of and making adjustments to our beliefs, we empower ourselves to re-evaluate our perceptions, thoughts, and feelings…and thereby our responses.

> *"Belief systems come with a warranty. If you don't like*
> *them, you can exchange them for ones you like."*
> —Bruce D Schneider

The real power that your beliefs have is the questions that they cause you to ask yourself. In NLP, the term Presupposition simply means that you pre suppose that something is true. So if you ask yourself, "Why do I always make mistakes"?, you are pre supposing as truth that mistakes always happen for you. With a question like that, backed up with such a belief, your destiny is, of course, predetermined. Instead, next time you think you made a mistake, try asking yourself what you can learn from the situation or how this lesson will prevent you from making a similar mistake in the future.

A limiting belief can also be a group belief. Group beliefs can create "social proof". This phenomena is when everyone believes information from the experts, so it is accepted as fact. For instance, the experts once declared that the world was flat and the sun revolved around the earth. What we can learn from all this is to question our beliefs and do not believe everything we think or hear. Bottom line…choose the beliefs that empower you to live the life you want, and question any belief that is not in full support of your chosen destiny.

> *"We are what we think. All that we are arises with our*
> *thoughts. With our thoughts…we make the world."*
> —Buddha

One more thought on beliefs:

Beliefs have the capacity to override the effects of drugs in the body. Studies in the science of psychoneuroimmunology (the mind-body relationship) have shown that our beliefs possibly play a more significant role than treatment. We all know about the placebo effect, but in a Harvard University study Dr. Henry Beecher did an experiment where 100 students were given either a stimulant or a barbiturate. The students given the stimulant were told they were given the barbiturate, and the students given the barbiturate were told they were given the stimulant. Half of the students had reactions to the drugs that were in line with their beliefs, the exact opposite of the chemical reactions the drugs produced in their bodies. Beecher stated that a drug's usefulness is a direct result of not only the chemical properties of the drug, but the patient's belief in the effectiveness and usefulness (thus showing the power of our thoughts).

Dr. Norman Cousins, author of the book "Anatomy of an Illness" recites that the moment a patient is diagnosed with an illness (has a label), the patient becomes worse. Labels like cancer and heart disease produce panic, leading to feelings of helplessness and even depression, which compromise the effectiveness of the body's immune system. How you react to events in your life can directly activate or suppress your immune response.

"Your immune system is constantly eavesdropping on your internal dialogue."
—Deepak Chopra

Now think about this…Let's say you received a blood transfusion and the doctor informed you that you contracted AIDS from the procedure, it was a full blown case, and you had six months to live. Also imagine that you believed him without question. What do you think would happen with your health during the next six months? It's scary to think about that, isn't it? Especially if he was mistaken.

2.6 THE MASK YOU WEAR TO KEEP YOU SAFE

Imagine yourself in the womb. Nice and safe. Relaxing on your heated waterbed and enjoying the room service. You have been here about nine months and, although you are feeling quite at home, things are starting to get a little cramped. Now, all of a sudden, some massive force is pushing you down a narrow path until you emerge into a room with bright lights and someone with a mask smacks your bottom.

Wow…after a start like that, no wonder you want to feel safe. Soon after, in order to gain approval from others, you learn to follow instructions and behave in a way that keeps you safe and rewards you with items or actions you desire.

Your behavior has been influenced by so many people…parents, childhood friends, siblings, teachers, TV and movie heroes, entertainers; the list goes on and on.

In your constant quest for approval, you start wearing a mask to show those that are important to you that you are exhibiting the behavior they want. Perhaps your mask is that you are so tough they better not mess with you. Or, you project a masquerade that you are perfect, enticing all to admire you. Did you put on the veil of niceness and cooperation so as to be well liked, or is your mask poor poor pitiful me?

The problem is that we forget we are wearing a mask, and we allow our cover to become our reality. Or, we strive to build a better and better mask. Instead, realize that what is under the veil and underneath your insecurities is a self that is whole, complete and perfect, just the way you are. The truth has always been there, waiting for you to discover it and take back your individual power and uniqueness.

> *"Now play the game…your game. The one you were meant to play.*
> *The one that was given to you when you came into this world."*
> —Bagger Vance

Realize there really is no true safety in this world. None of us get out of here alive. So stop looking for safety, take off the mask, and be the emotionally fit self that you were meant to be.

> *"Avoidance of risk is no safer in the long run than outright exposure, Life is either a daring adventure, or nothing."*
> —Helen Keller

And while you're at it, put down this book and take some time to not improve, change, or "fix" yourself. Just go do whatever you enjoy doing or be with whomever you enjoy being with for a while. There is nothing you need to change, do, or be in order to achieve happiness. You can just, right now...step into BEing happy. Go ahead...I'll be here when you get back.

> *"Be yourself. There is nothing more for you to do than to be the best YOU that you can be - with no imitation, no pretense, no guilt, no shame."*
> —Jonathan Lockwood Huie

> *"Who you are is someone who asked to be dropped off on Earth so you could do something remarkable, something that matters to you that you* couldn't do *anywhere, any when else"*
> —Richard Bach

2.7 THE "VOICE" IN YOUR HEAD

Did you ever notice that there is a voice in your head that talks incessantly? It argues with itself and has an opinion about everything. And it never stops. Have you ever just sat back and observed the voice, or do you identify with the voice and think it is you?

"What voice? There is no voice in my head. Maybe I should put this book down and get a pizza? Nah, I want to eat healthier. But a pizza would taste so good. I don't feel like driving, and delivery gets cold. I need to drive to work anyway. My job is really getting annoying. What's with Bob's attitude lately? Maybe I should find somewhere else to work. I wonder why Mary didn't call me back? I was noticing some attitude from her. Maybe things have run their course with her. I should just blow the whole thing off." And on and on it goes. Imagine if you had a friend that you took with you everywhere and your friend spoke the same way as your voice. How long would you keep this friend around? Yet…most of the time you listen to this voice and believe what it says.

> *"Ninety nine percent of your thoughts are a complete waste of time.*
> *They do nothing but freak you out."*
> —Michael Singer

The voice, which is simply an expression of your unconscious programming, does not care about being in harmony with what is actually happening in the world; it only wants the world outside to be in harmony with itself. To achieve this, the voice is constantly using thoughts to create a running commentary about how the world outside of you should be. The voice, in its attempt to control reality and neutralize any disturbance inside of you, will continually sound off about what is right and what is wrong with every person and situation. This incessant chatter is driven by fear and desire; the fear that you will not receive what you desire, and also the fear that you will get what you do not desire.

Your voice is also trying to protect you from scars left by negative events; things that happened throughout your life which have left wounds on your psyche. When a person or event triggers a negative memory, it causes a disturbance inside of you. (More about "pushing your buttons" in chapter 4, Your Unconscious Mind). When this happens, your voice struggles to rationalize and justify... and to prove that you are right and the situation or other person wrong.

Consider all the chatter the mind creates when an event happens that is not in harmony with the way you *think* things should occur. In fact, anytime something happens which creates a disturbance inside of you, the voice will try to rationalize the event in order to negate the disturbance. And what about when you act on the message the voice is creating and you externalize the internal disturbance? The outward expression of this internal disturbance can often be anger and violence. Just like your body will attempt to purge itself if you eat bad food, your mind will also try to purge the bad energy. Look around and observe all the troubles that are caused by the outward expression of inner disturbances. Ask yourself...Am I directing my thoughts or are my thoughts directing me?

> *"Thought creates your world and then says 'I didn't do it'"*
> —David Bohm

Try this for a day: be aware of everything the voice is saying as if it is another person. The voice is going to talk, that's what it does, your job is to not get pulled in. Don't try to stop it from talking or change what it says, just be aware of it. Stay centered and relax into the awareness. Imagine it is not you, it is another being. "Big me" is the awareness, and "little me" is the voice. Listen to little me languish on and on about everything. Little me is very melodramatic. Watch how little me makes constant judgments about everything and has a running critique about the world around you. When you try this experiment, you will realize that you have only had one problem your entire life.

> *"Ya see this guy right here staring back at you (in the mirror). That's your toughest opponent. Every time you get into the ring, that's who your goin' against. I believe that in boxing and I believe that in life."*
> —Rocky Balboa

Accept what is happening despite the voice incessantly chattering and making judgments. In the chapter on Stress, we discussed judgments being the main cause of stress. The ego is constantly judging. Remember this: Events are reality, and your resistance to reality is what can transform these events into personal problems. It is actually possible to never have another problem for the rest of your life, by dealing with events and the reality of the situation instead of your own fears and desires. When you have calmed your fears and desires, you will have calmed the voice.

The moment you become aware of the voice instead of identifying with the voice ...that is when you will find your escape from the dilemma of the minds incessant chatter. Right now, your life is not your own. It belongs to the voice. Take it back. What you will find is that your will is stronger than the voice. You just have to exercise this power of will. Remember, do not try to stop the voice or change the voice, just stop identifying with what the voice is saying.

What will happen is you will start to see life as it is instead of being ruled by your inner disturbances. You will be aware of the events actually occurring, and as a result will be stronger at everything you do. You will be consciously choosing where your attention should resonate. Interacting with the world outside of you will take the place of reacting to an internal disturbance, and your whole life will change.

"What a liberation to realize that the 'voice in my head' is not who I am. Who am I then? The one who see's that."
—Eckhart Tolle

The voice in your head strongly influences your self-image, which is discussed in the next chapter.

2.8 YOUR SELF-IMAGE

Your self-image, or self-esteem, is basically the perception you have of yourself. The way you view your identity, your abilities, your self-worth, your looks, etc. becomes your reality, regardless of the truth. The self-picture you have painted will create the outcome you expect, because the outcome you expect is based on how you see yourself.

Your self-image is primarily based on your early childhood experiences and the embarrassment, shame, and confusion that came with the challenges of your adolescent years. If you are lucky, it is also made up of some positive memories reflecting good things you have done and successes you experienced. Unfortunately, for most of us the bad outweighs the good, and our self-image is largely the result of accidental interpretations and inaccurate memories.

> *"Life does not consist mainly - or even largely — of facts*
> *and happenings. It consists mainly of the storm of thoughts*
> *that is forever blowing through one's head."*
> —Mark Twain

Your self-image regulates everything you think, feel, and do... automatically. It is one of the most vital programs in your unconscious.

If your self-esteem is not healthy, the quality of your choices will reflect that. Your intuition will interpret information in a way that is harmful, such as imagining that all incidents directly relate to you. A healthy self-esteem allows you to detach and not take everything so personally. It allows you to step outside in a light hearted and easy going manner.

> *"No amount of self improvement can make up for a lack of self acceptance."*
> —Y.J. Peretson

If you have ever attempted something that was more than your usual, only to find yourself backing down or giving up, it is because your self-image was operating within the range of your predetermined limits. You quit because deep down inside it didn't feel like something you could or would do.

If you have ever made a statement like, "That's just who I am" or "that's not who I am." or "I'm just not that kind of person"...it was your self- image operating behind the scene.

Think about all the limiting things we heard as children, some said directly to us and some overheard in talk between our parents or other adults. We are kind of like the elephants at the circus. Have you ever seen these huge animals tethered to a post by a little piece of rope? Have you ever wondered why they don't just pull out the post or snap the small rope, and then just walk away? The elephants do not walk away because that small rope is their "limit", and they learned about this limit when they were young. When an elephant is a baby, it is tied to a big post with a huge rope and chain. When the elephant's mother moves away from the baby and the baby tries to follow, it is stopped short by the rope. It pulls and pulls, but there is no give to the big rope, so there is absolutely no chance the baby elephant can break loose. After a while, the elephant ceases trying, and then the trainers can use a smaller and smaller rope, and a weaker and weaker post.

As you have probably heard, elephants have very good memories. They learn as babies that when they are tethered to a post they are stuck. So... adult elephants live within the boundaries that they accepted as baby elephants.

We humans have good memories, too. The boundaries that were set when we were small are the boundaries that we are tethered to as adults. We can break free if we choose to, but most of us accept our limits as real.

Make it a habit to listen for the voice in your head that causes you to hesitate when trying something out of your comfort zone. If you hear that voice telling you that you are in over your head, do not identify with the voice, just be aware of it. If it is not your adult voice of reason, but just some scary noises from your past, simply do not give any energy to the voice, and allow it to fade away.

An old Cherokee told his grandson "My Son, there is a battle between two wolves inside of us all. One is evil. It is anger, jealousy, greed, resentment, inferiority, lies, and ego. The other is good. It is joy, peace, love, hope, humility, kindness, empathy, and truth." The boy thought about it and asked "Which wolf wins?" The old man quietly replied "The one you feed."

41

Another paralyzing source of limitation is body image. Do you compare your body to some ideal model? Are you frustrated to watch your body age? Consider a loved one that is aging. Do you judge them so harshly? We criticize our bodies when we objectify them, or see them as objects that should be a certain way. Much healthier for our psyches is to instead personify our body, or see it as a person. Accept your body as you would any relationship you care about and love. Be considerate of your body...see things from its viewpoint. Strengthen and take care of your body, not from your ego's point of view, but from your body's perspective. When you feel "I am enough" the world will be enough. But if you feel "I am not enough" the world will never be sufficient.

"Our self image, strongly held, essentially determines what we become."
—Dr. Maxwell Maltz

The key to changing self-image is to choose the type of self image we would like to have, and then gather evidence to support that belief. Of the over 200 million bits of information out there every second, isn't it time to select the 200 bits that support your self image choice? Start seeing yourself as the person you have chosen. What posture would a person with that self image display? What facial expression? What thoughts would he be thinking? How would she treat others? What words would she speak? What would he believe about himself and the world around him?

It is important to keep in mind that the key to all lasting change is repetition. By adjusting the images in our mind, we change how we feel. Doing this over and over again is like water running over the ground. Pretty soon it will create a path, then a river...and a new neuro-pathway will be formed in your mind. Keep this river metaphor in mind for all behavioral changes. Picture your old neuro-pathway as a river. When you go to a motivational seminar and are inspired to change, the water is redirected to a better ground, searching for a new channel. The reason that you revert to your old behavior a few days later is because a new channel was not created and so the water drifted back into the old river, or old pattern. The key to change is to consciously create new neuro-pathways, or a new river...and be sure that the water is permanently diverted. This is done through repetition, ideally for a minimum of 21 days.

Within 21 days, a new neuro pathway is formed; like a narrow, shallow river bed. However, according to P. Murali Doraiswamy M.D., member of the Duke Institute for Brain Sciences, completely breaking bad habits and establishing good ones usually takes 12 weeks.

"That's because the brain needs time to reconfigure its soft wiring. It does this by establishing new network connections and resetting your pleasure thresholds." Dr. Doraiswamy is using real time brain imaging to pinpoint how lifestyle changes can alter the brains' networks.

Make sure the water flows to the new path for 3 weeks, and it will then be easy to keep it flowing in that direction for 9 more weeks. Pretty soon, the old river will dry up, weeds will grow, and fertile ground around the new river will flourish.

> *"People tell me that motivation doesn't last…*
> *and I tell them…neither does bathing, that's why I do it every day."*
> —Zig Ziglar

> *"Some things you have to do every day. Eating seven apples on Saturday*
> *night instead of one a day just isn't going to get the job done."*
> —Jim Rohn

We must take the time and put forth the effort to create new neuro-pathways deeper than the old ones. When we start thinking, acting and behaving in an empowering way, we are rewarded with outcomes that we want, naturally and automatically, and these in turn reinforce our new self-image. Our whole relationship with life upgrades in the process. Will this take some time? Of course it will. Will this take some continued effort? Absolutely. Will it be worth it? You better believe it will!

> *"The self-image is the key to human personality and human behavior.*
> *Change the self-image and you change the personality and the behavior."*
> —Maxwell Maltz

2.9 NUTRITIONAL HEALTH

We are all on a diet. A diet is simply your eating habits. Some diets are more beneficial to health and well being than others. If you go on a diet to achieve a goal, then achieve the goal and "go back to normal", the diet has not changed anything. However, when you contemplate your body as energy, and you see the food you ingest as energy, it is easier to choose foods for good health and proper weight. Make the food you eat a conscious choice, not something ruled by habit. If you generate food choices from an utmost respect for this miracle that is your body, your weight will be at a healthy level, as will your energy and general health. The real point here is to take care of and respect your body.

The raw food and the macrobiotic diets both consist of healthy eating habits. The raw diet consists of uncooked food, and the macrobiotic diet is comprised of all cooked food. Both are good. Both are healthy, yet they are opposite. Which one is better? Expert opinions differ. Experts also disagree on whether dairy is good or bad for you. How about animal protein? Again, which expert are you asking? How about coffee? Red wine? A simple answer is that what works for one person may not be best for another. We all have different sensitivities, tolerances, and body types. You know best how different foods make you feel. Maybe you get tired and lethargic after certain foods. Perhaps certain foods cause you to feel light and energetic. Be aware of your energy levels after eating and choose to create eating habits that work for you. In fact, if you ask yourself the following two questions and obey the answers, your quality of life will immediately improve. What should you eat less of because you feel tired or sluggish? What should you eat more of to feel energized and healthy?

A person who is overweight and "can't" lose the weight is simply asking themselves the wrong questions. Instead of "What would fill me up" or "what would taste the best?", a better question is "What is most healthy and would make me feel good?" or "What is something light and tasty that would give me good energy?"

A healthy balanced diet energizes and fortifies your entire body. With an energized body, emotional fitness arrives easier and more naturally… because all of our parts work synergistically.

Man may be the captain of his fate, but is also the victim of his blood sugar."
—Wilfrid G. Oakley

A crucial component to keep in your awareness is that disease is a condition caused by the human mind. Illness, however, is a natural and human experience. When you are sick, ill, or injured; envision it as just one more human experience that will help you grow.

"The body, like everything else in life, is a mirror of our inner thoughts.
The body is always talking to us, if we will only take the time to listen.
Every cell within your body responds to every single
thought you think and every word you speak."
—Louise Hay

What we put in our bodies has a dramatic effect on our mental health. If you would like to learn more about using foods to do naturally what certain drugs try to do artificially, I suggest *Fire your Doctor by* Andrew Saul. If you desire to learn about the effect of food on your internal organs, and in turn your emotions, you may want to read *"Emotional Wisdom"* by Mantak Chia and Dena Saxer, where specific foods are recommended to alleviate different negative emotions.

Your directive is to choose foods that make you feel good, light, and energetic, while choosing thoughts and beliefs that allow you to experience happiness...it's that simple. Bottom line...good nutrition and disease prevention is about more than just the food you eat. It is based on the thoughts you think.

When you step on a scale, remember that the scale will not tell you how great a person you are, how much people love you, that you are amazing in ways a scale could not even begin to measure, and that you have the power within you to choose happiness. Furthermore, your greatness is not found on a scale, in the mirror, in a classroom, from reading books such as this one, or from flattering comments from friends, family members, or lovers. Your greatness is within you, so be conscious of the potential that flows through you...and have gratitude for all of the beauty you harbor inside.

"It's not where you are today that counts. It's where you are headed."
—Arthur F. Lenehan

3. VALUES & NEEDS

Our values influence our needs and our needs may, in turn, influence our values. Because of this, our needs and values can be so intertwined that it is difficult to distinguish whether we are talking about a need or a value. Sometimes we should question our values if they stem from behavioral conditioning and have created a need that is not in harmony with our best interest. The goal of this chapter is to help you understand your values and needs, so that you become aware of the best choices for you.

Values are deep, unconscious belief systems that drive our behavior. We construct a set of values for issues that are important to us, for who we want to be, for what we desire, and for the lengths we are willing to go to obtain what we want...the list goes on. We are a product of our value system. Examples of values are listed in the table below.

Type of Value	Value
What is important to us	Happiness, Self-Awareness, Self-mastery, Fulfillment, Consciousness, Spirituality, Experience, Excellence, etc.
What we want	Abundance, Security, Relationships, Romance, Health, Fitness, Education, Appearance, Achievement, Personal or Professional Growth, Friendship, Family, Peace of mind, etc.
How we will get what we want	Creativity, Authenticity, Loyalty, Being Orderly, Respectfulness, Trust, Openness, Humility, Honesty, Compassion, Caring, Balance, Gratitude, etc.

There are many more values than listed above. The purpose of the list is to start you thinking about YOUR values. When you honor your values, your actions will be in harmony with what is important to you.

Your values change with context. For example, you probably have certain values for what you want in a relationship and other values for what you aspire to in a job.

Your values can also change over time. You might arrive at the end of your quest for more money, cars, homes, outfits...and may come to realize that more money does not equate to a better life, and consequently your values will change, and also your needs.

When making important decisions, imagine looking back on your choices through the eyes of your future self. Look back from 1 year, 5 years, or maybe even 20 or 30 years in the future. Now...looking back through the eyes of your future self, ask how your present choice has affected you. What needs and values did you honor? Which did you violate? Using this method provides a new and enhanced perspective.

"We are free up to the point of choice, then the choice controls the chooser."
—Mary Crowley

At a Tony Robbins seminar I attended, Mr. Robbins told the audience that, according to Human Needs Psychology, human beings have six basic needs (see table below). He stated that people will go to great lengths to meet their essential needs, even if the actions are destructive.

Need	Type of Need	Definition
Certainty	Essential	The need to be comfortable and have consistency and security in our relationships
Uncertainty	Essential	Once certainty has been met, the need to seek variety, challenges, what's fresh, new, and exciting.
Significance	Essential	The need to feel wanted, needed, important, and worthy of love
Love	Essential	The need to feel love and be connected to others
Growth	Spiritual	The need to keep developing ourselves and our world
Contribution	Spiritual	The need to go beyond our needs and give to others.

> *"Uncertainty is the only certainty there is, and knowing*
> *how to live with insecurity is the only security."*
> —John Allen Paulos

Significance manifests high on the list for most people as we all want to feel important. Sometimes, in their hunger for significance, people may attempt to obtain it in the wrong way, by making others feel insignificant. The best way to become significant is by helping others to grow in importance. A crucial aspect in emotional growth is to learn to receive gracefully, honoring another person's need for contribution as well as significance. Sure...it's nice to give to others, but it can be an act of love (for both people) to gracefully let others do for you. Has your need to feel significant kept you from allowing others to feel important by not accepting their contributions or their expressions of love?

> *"You can get anything you want in life,*
> *if you'll just help enough other people get what they want."*
> —Zig Ziglar

Are you motivated by your values or by your needs? Often people override their values to meet their needs when the need is perceived as more important. For example, a person who treasures honesty but is hungry and has no money may be motivated to steal food. Or someone who values growth may hesitate to take action because they are fearful of what the growth entails. A person who values excellence on the job but is obsessed about the need to get something done on time may compromise the value to meet the need. Fear is often the catalyst that will cause a need to override a value.

The importance of each of our needs and values is forever changing. We seek certainty, but when we have it, we may get bored and want adventure (uncertainty). We seek growth, but then reach a point where we just want stability. We may seek to give...but then long to focus more on ourselves. The real key is to be aware, and make choices that are mindful and in harmony with our needs and values.

> *"Happiness is that state of consciousness which proceeds*
> *from the achievement of one's values."*
> —Ayn Rand

3.1 RELATIONSHIPS

Have you ever wondered why there are so many misunderstandings and conflicts in our relationships with others? This chapter will help you understand why, and empower you to make changes for the better.

We constantly get input from our senses. From this information comes pictures, sounds, feelings, tastes, and smells that we then blend together in our unconscious to create perceptions. Some of these perceptions of current experience may be from memories, fantasies, or plans that we think of for only an instant. In fact, what we perceive is happening at any given moment is probably made up mostly of internal thought activity rather than what is actually occurring.

We have discussed that our thoughts affect our emotions and our bodies, and our bodies affect our emotions and thoughts...a cycle that continues endlessly.

Now...consider what happens when two human beings interact. Each one is in the grip of a mind-body-mind cycle, and now they are also affecting each other. For example, a person may have a particular meaning for what they are saying, but their listener may attach a completely different meaning to what they are hearing. Is it any wonder there are so many misunderstandings?

"I know you believe you understood what you think I said,
but I am not sure you realize that what you heard is not what I meant."
—John Sorensen

Humans are always seeking love. We search for other humans to give us love because we do not understand that all the love we will ever need is within ourselves. If we share the love that is already within us, we will find something so much better than we would find by searching for love.

"If each of us could love ourselves as we wish to be loved,
then we wouldn't let our hunger for love make decisions for us."
—Don Miguel Ruiz

A person might begin a relationship to fulfill a need, such as loneliness, and will often find that the relationship does not satisfy this need. The possibility of a healthy relationship is greatly increased when it is started not for a need, but instead for a want.

- Interdependence is when you are with someone because you want (want is a positive emotion).
- Co-dependence is when you are with someone because you need (need is a negative emotion), and you exist to need and be needed.

In romantic movies, the expression "you complete me" is often glorified. In reality, if you are looking for another person to "complete you", the relationship will not be as strong and satisfying as it would if you became "complete" on your own and shared your fulfillment with the other person.

One key to a healthy relationship is sharing, and we cannot share what we do not already have. We cannot expect a relationship to magically instill within us the peace, contentment, and love which we have failed to establish within ourselves. If you do not love yourself, you will be challenged to fully love someone else.

However, you can have a need for love, and if there is someone who needs you, that is what we sometimes call love. Unfortunately though, this may not be real love. It could be possessiveness, it may be control with no respect, it is possibly addictive clinging that can turn into hate within a second, but it is rarely true love.

With the challenges of relationships and life in general, most people are walking around with blocked energy in their heart and other energy centers (Chakras). Sometimes all we need to do is open up our energy centers and set ourselves free from the prison of past conditioning. Start by accepting yourself for who you are and stop rejecting or judging yourself for any reason. You have the right to love, smile, and be happy. So share your love, and don't be afraid to receive love either.

"Learning to love yourself, that is the greatest love of all…"
—George Benson

Your relationships are a reflection of your relationship with yourself. Unresolved issues from past relationships will surface in the next one…and the next one…and the next one.

"The people we are in relationships with are always a mirror, reflecting back our own beliefs, and simultaneously we are mirrors, reflecting back their beliefs. So, relationship is one of the most powerful tools for growth. If we look honestly at our relationships, we can see how much we have created them."
—Shakti Gawain

Every relationship presents you another piece of information about yourself. Ask yourself…Why am I in a relationship? Why do I even want one? Take the time to answer these questions.

In Dr. Gary Chapman's book *The Five Love Languages: The Secret to Love That Lasts (www.5lovelanguages.com)*, he explains that there are five love languages that we utilize to communicate with each other in relationships. These love languages are explained in the following table:

Love Language	What You Want
Words of Affirmation	If this is your language, hearing nice words means everything to you, and hearing the wrong words, like insults, hurts you deeply.
Quality Time	I've heard it said that the way to spell love to a child is T I M E. Well, for some adults, your undivided attention means everything.
Gifts	If this is your love language, it is the thought and effort behind the gift that means so much to you. A missed special occasion would be devastating for someone with this need.
Acts of Service	The nicest thing you can say to a person with this need is "Let me do that for you". Broken commitments are devastating for this type of person.
Physical Touch	Not just sex…but any kind of touch, such as a pat on the back, holding hands, and just being present… means so much to this type of person.

I was at a life coaching seminar which focused on the teachings of Dr. Gary Chapman and the five love languages. The presenter mentioned that, as a child, she expressed love through touch and affection just like her father, whereas her mother and brother showed love through acts of service. Because she was unaware of this theory, she felt loved by her father but unloved by her mother and brother. As an adult and after learning from Chapman's teachings about the different love languages we all possess, she now remembers how her mother and brother were always doing acts of service for her. She realizes now that they were expressing love in their way. In fact, they may not have felt loved by her, because she did not express love the same way they did.

After her talk, I approached her and expressed how much I had enjoyed the talk. As she thanked me, someone close by said "Hey Gary...words of affirmation just don't do it for her". I realized this person was being quite insightful, so I gave her a hug as I thanked her for the presentation. The positive difference was very obvious in her reaction.

What can we learn from this? Every interaction with another human being is a relationship, and each person may speak a different love language. If you have a boss that likes to award gifts, but you prefer words of affirmation, a disconnect will occur, because your boss is showing appreciation but you are not feeling it. Similarly, if your husband shows love through touch and you desire acts of service, you may feel like saying "quit pawing at me and do something to help around the house." Or, if the reverse is true, you might complain "all you ever do is fix things around the house but you never show me any love and affection".

"How can a woman be expected to be happy with a man who insists on treating her as if she were a perfectly normal human being."
—Oscar Wilde

One of my clients experienced a lot of problems in her marriage until she realized that she values quality time, and her husband showed his love through gifts. He was always working and buying her presents, yet all she wanted was to spend some quality time together. Through her realization of their different love languages, she no longer feels un-loved, and is now able to perceive his love clearly. With the power to understand comes the power to change. For her, the following quote truly applies:

"Rings and jewels are not gifts, but apologies for gifts.
The only gift is a portion of thyself."
—Ralph Waldo Emerson

Needs, values, and love languages play a big role in relationships and are interdependent upon each other in their creation of the best possible harmony between two people. When you are with a partner, friend, or anyone with whom you are close, be aware of their most important needs and values and how they prefer these to be fulfilled. For example, if you have a partner who values significance, is it in your nature to encourage others to feel significant? Does he/she crave words of affirmation and would offering affirmations on a regular basis be something you would be happy and comfortable doing?

Do you have similar ideas and aspirations when it comes to growth? How about contribution or service? Perhaps the values between you and your partner are different, but are those differences easily accepted or, better yet, admired?

"If (s)he's an apple and you're an orange, celebrate your
differences - make a great fruit salad. Love isn't about being
the same - it's about being sweet with each other."
—Jonathan Lockwood Huie

If you are in a relationship that is less than fulfilling, it may boil down to something really simple.

After deciding you are fully committed to fixing your relationship, start by looking inward. Become aware of any issues within yourself that you are expecting a relationship to satisfy, and determine if your expectations are part of the problem. It is your responsibility to contribute a fullness of spirit to the relationship.

"Do not seek fulfillment through work or intimacy.
Be already full. Work and intimacy are opportunities to share your gift,
and be vanished in the bliss of the giving."
—David Deida

Share your needs, values, and love languages with your partner to gain an idea as to the change that might be needed. As you are venturing forward, please bear in mind that people either want visual (show me), auditory (tell me), or kinesthetic(touch me or demonstrate to me) demonstrations of love.

Most relationship problems are quite simple. Communicate with your partner and agree on the way forward to mutual happiness, without violating any needs or values. As you move ahead, remember that the path to success is rarely a straight line. The important thing is to understand that you don't have to do much to start moving your relationship in a more satisfying direction.

The final step is giving. Try to give unconditionally, before any thought of receiving...and do this from a place of gratitude. Incredibly, when you take responsibility for a relationship, more often than not, the other person quickly chooses to take responsibility as well.

"I have come to the frightening conclusion that I am the decisive element. It is my personal approach that creates the climate. It is my daily mood that makes the weather. I possess tremendous power to make life miserable or joyous. I can be a tool of torture or an instrument of inspiration. I can humiliate or humor, hurt or heal. In all situations, it is my response that decides whether a crisis is escalated or de-escalated, and a person is humanized or de-humanized."
—Goethe

We talk a lot in this book about asking yourself the right questions. "What do I love the most about this person?" will serve you a lot better than "How could they keep doing that thing which annoys me? It is your choice to ask empowering questions or disempowering questions. (more on questions in the chapter: Talk to Yourself)

Is your partner your "ball and chain" or your "lover"? The way you refer to your partner creates a mental representation of them in your mind. "My better half" is a better portrayal than "the old bag". These verbal images (nicknames) may start out innocently enough, but over time they affect the way you see and feel about that person.

"When you meet your friend on the roadside or in the marketplace, let the spirit in you move your lips and direct your tongue. Let the voice within your voice speak to the ear of his ear."
—Kahlil Gibran

It is very important to understand that negative emotions will not exist when you are in a state of gratitude. When you find something for which to be grateful, and make that your focus, your appreciation continues to climb. Try it…the only thing you have to lose is pain.

> *"With gratitude, all life appears as a blessing - without gratitude, all of life is perceived as a burden."*
> —Jonathan Lockwood Huie

> *"Whenever you're in conflict with someone, there is one factor that can make the difference between damaging your relationship and deepening it. That factor is attitude."*
> —William James

One more word on relationships…all of your relationships. It is not your job to make anyone else happy…and it is not anyone else's job to bring you happiness. Often we take our loved one's unhappiness personally, even when it has nothing to do with us. We jump through hoops and sacrifice things that matter to us in an attempt to make them happy. Women will devote themselves as if on a mission to make their man happy. Men will bend over backwards to give everything to their wives in the hope of an attitude adjustment. Parents will cater to their child's every whim in a vain attempt to increase his or her enjoyment. I have never seen anyone become happy as a result of these actions, have you? Self centered, maybe… dependent, probably…temporarily elated, possibly. But happy? Rarely or never. This is because happiness is not something that can be given from one person to another, and it is certainly not something you can "Make" another person become. Happiness is earned when an individual embraces all the good that life has to offer, and chooses the meaning they want to attach to events in the world.

> *"Nobody owes nobody nothin'. You owe yourself."*
> —Rocky Balboa

Another problem with trying to make someone happy is that eventually the "giver" becomes resentful when the attempts fail. Now that doesn't mean you should not care about the feelings of others. Of course you should. Offer support and love to those you care about, as long as you realize that the responsibility for being happy lies with each individual. Support your loved ones in their quest for joy, but never believe that you are the grantor of it. Most importantly, never believe that someone else is responsible for your happiness.

"If you want others to be happy, practice compassion.
If you want to be happy, practice compassion."
—Dalai Lama

Earlier in this chapter I stated: If you are looking for someone to "complete you", do not expect a strong or satisfying relationship. Instead, become "complete" on your own and share your fulfillment. The whole world can love you, but that love will not create your happiness. What will make you happy is the love flowing through you and the love you share. You can have the relationship that fulfills your dreams, but you must begin with you. It's up to you, it's not up to anyone else.

"Relationship is an art. The dream that two create is more difficult to master than one. To keep the two of you happy, you have to keep your half perfect."
—Don Miguel Ruiz – The Mastery of Love

"Give your hearts, but not to each other's keeping. For only the hand of life can keep your hearts. And stand together, but not too near together: For the pillars of a temple stand apart, and the oak tree and the cypress grow not in each other's shadows."
—Kahlil Gibran

"And in the end, the love you take, is equal to the love you make."
—Lennon/McCartney

3.2 IT'S TOO LATE

What do you do when the relationship is over? The same teachings apply. Be happy that you were able to spend time together and appreciate the growth from your experiences. We learn vast amounts about ourselves through our relationships, so appreciate the education you received. Know that when a relationship has run its course, it is the perfect time to move on. Finally, understand that the relationship was a good fit for the person you were during the special moments you shared.

> *"Don't cry because it's over, smile because it happened."*
> —Luke Dawson

If you are angry or resentful, you are simply at battle with what is. Life is simple...reality exists and you decide how to interact with it. If you treat life like it is a battle, then war is an inevitable result. Try instead to accept reality and move forward towards your contentment.

> *"If you cry because the sun has gone out of your life,*
> *your tears will prevent you from seeing the stars."*
> —Rabindranath Tagore

We are all behaving as best we can based on our level of consciousness and mental capacity. All we want is happiness. Why, then, would you allow anger to surface when someone does not live up to your expectations?

There are only two possible reasons. Either you want to punish them, or you want to blame them. And if that is the case, you are asking yourself the wrong questions. By asking the right questions, you immediately change your focus and, therefore, how you feel.

> *"The mark of your ignorance is the depth of your*
> *belief in injustice and tragedy.*
> *What the caterpillar calls the end of the world...*
> *The master calls a butterfly."*
> —Richard Bach

"Staying with someone who doesn't appreciate you is like
standing in quick sand, slowly sinking in sadness."
—M.J. Young

"Never chase love, attention, or affection.
If they aren't given freely, they aren't worth having."
—C.G. Richter

"If she doesn't want your gift, your deepest wisdom,
your unsuppressed loving, then why would you want to be with her?
—David Deida

If overcoming anger is your primary issue, go back and re-read the earlier chapters about emotional fitness, such as *Your Energy, Overcoming Victim and Conflict Energy,* or *Understanding Anger.*

"I have decided to stick with love. Hate is too great a burden to bear."
—Martin Luther King, Jr.

"Every situation, properly perceived, becomes an opportunity to heal."
—A Course in Miracles

If you still have a grudge and are unable to forgive, perhaps this message from the book *Contentment* by Robert A. Johnson and Jerry M. Ruhl may help:

"We have utilized numerous psychological tools to try to facilitate
forgiveness, but in the end it seems that most people are not willing to
let go until they have something more important to move on to."

Decide what is most important in your life… harboring a grudge or being happy…and then move on.

May I suggest you move on to the next chapter? It will give you a greater understanding of this complex and wondrous machine that I call me and you call you…

4. YOUR UNCONSCIOUS MIND

*I*n this book, I have chosen to use the term unconscious mind to represent all of the programming which resides in your subconscious. To be clear, the conscious, unconscious and subconscious are not separate subdivisions, but are interdependent factions of your mind. (In our society, the terms subconscious mind and unconscious mind are used interchangeably). To illustrate, see your subconscious mind as the miracle that knows how to perform such amazing feats like coordinating the muscles that you are using to hold this book and turn its pages. Do you consciously know how to synchronize your muscles to sit up, read, and turn the page? You don't have to, because your subconscious mind is accomplishing these actions, while pumping your heart, circulating your blood, and completing all of the other miraculous events that you do on a daily basis without any effort at all. Your subconscious is your perfection, your inner guide, your teacher, your higher self.

The unconscious mind is the portion of our subconscious that controls all of the programming from birth onward. It is our habits and our reactive self, the part of us that responds without thinking. It is a repository of stimulus response tapes that are derived from learned experiences. Like a computer, your unconscious accepts the programming without any judgments about whether it is helpful or harmful. It remembers the feeling, not the event, except that the feeling reminds your conscious mind of the event. In other words: The unconscious is an emotionless database of stored beliefs and programs which makes no judgments, similar to the programming in your computer. When a certain stimulus is received, a certain program will activate.

Your conscious mind, the seat of your personal identity or ego, is your thinking mind. It contains your dreams and aspirations. It is the part of your mind that reviews the past, dwells on the future, and disconnects from the present. This is also the part of the mind that solves problems and "thinks". It is imperative to train your conscious mind to ponder only what you want to create, because your conscious mind feeds your unconscious mind.

According to a 2005 article in U.S. News & World report titled "Mysteries of the Mind: Your Unconscious is Making your Everyday

Decisions" by Marianne Szegedy-Maszak, when it comes to neurological processing abilities, the unconscious mind is more than one million times more powerful than the conscious mind. In addition, the programs acquired by the unconscious mind shape 95% or more of our life experiences.

We think we are consciously running our lives, but since our unconscious operates without conscious involvement, we can be completely unaware that our unconscious mind is influencing our decision making process. It is unconscious programming and belief systems that cause two people who experience the same situation to react in dramatically different ways.

Your unconscious mind can be your greatest asset or your worst liability. If you remain unaware of your mind's power, your life will be basically a printout of your unconscious programming. This programming was created when you were young, and acquired from others, or was acquired by your interpretation of events happening around you. Consequently, your reality is possibly being operated by the interpretations made by you as a 2 year old. The majority of these programs are limiting and disempowering.

*"Traditions are the guideposts driven deep in our subconscious minds.
The most powerful ones are those we can't even describe, aren't even aware of."*
—Ellen Goodman

The reason that we acquire most of our programs by the age of seven is because young children live in a hypnotic state. Between birth and 2 years old the brain operates at its lowest frequency (0.5 to 4 cycles per second), called delta waves. Between ages 2 and 6 a child's brain operates at theta (4 to 8 cycles per second). Hypnotists strive to drop brain activity to theta level because this frequency is the most suggestible, programmable state.

As stated earlier, when a certain stimulus is received, it activates a particular program. If you have ever found yourself getting upset over something that, if looked at logically, was quite trivial, you have experienced this stimulus response. This is commonly known as having "your buttons pushed". Buttons also get pushed if you have pain inside of you from something that happened in your past. For example, an irrational reaction in response to shouting may derive from a childhood wound. A metaphor for this pain response button is as follows: if I poked your shoulder, it probably would not hurt. However, if you had an open wound on your shoulder, it would hurt significantly, and the more severe the wound, the higher the pain level. The degree of your irritation lets you know the severity of the wound within you.

So when your buttons are activated, realize it is not what is happening on the outside, but what is happening within you. Next time someone "pushes your buttons", instead of blaming them...be thankful for the opportunity to know what your "buttons" are, so you can work through them to modify the stimulus response.

When you find yourself reacting to a pre-programmed trigger (button), first stop and take a deep breath. Then examine how you are interpreting the situation to cause this reaction. Inquire, as if you were an uninvolved observer, what is really taking place, and if there is another possible explanation. Maybe ask yourself what might be occurring for the other person in that moment. Imagine stepping into their shoes and perceiving the situation through their eyes. Then, when you are no longer emotional, analyze if there is a better way to handle a similar situation if it arises again.

I once worked with a client who claimed her husband always pushed her buttons. As she explained a specific incident that really angered her, I asked her to imagine what might have been going on for him and how he might have been feeling. She sat still for a moment, and then started to speak with compassion about what he must have been experiencing, and how insecure he must have felt at the time. I asked what she would now do in a similar situation after seeing things from his point of view. She smiled and said "I'd get up and rub his shoulders".

Through self awareness...you can always ask "Is this the reality I want to create within myself, or is it pre-programming?" Then decide if you want to accept your interpretation, or change it.

"There are no facts, only interpretations."
—Friedrich Nietzsche

4.1 TRAINING YOUR MIND

When you are in the process of learning, your actions are conscious, and once the process of learning is complete, these actions relocate to your unconscious. An example is when you learned to tie your shoes or learned to drive. There are some downsides to this; all of us have witnessed some drivers who would be well served by a return to consciousness.

"It is only through your conscious mind that you can reach the subconscious. Your conscious mind is the porter at the door, the watchman at the gate. It is to the conscious mind that the subconscious looks for all its impressions."
—Robert Collier

As discussed throughout this book, we learn through the quality of the questions that we are asked and that we ask ourselves. You also know that your unconscious is much more powerful than your conscious. Therefore, questions that keep you in your conscious mind are not as powerful as questions that access your unconscious. When you are thinking, you are in your conscious mind. Feelings and emotions are the key to your unconscious. As a life coach, I will ask you "what" questions to bring you into your feelings. If I ask you "why" questions, you are transported to your intellect (conscious mind), in order to defend yourself. For example, if you are executing some unwanted behavior and I ask "Why are you doing that"? You will respond with your intellect to answer the question, tell me your story, and maybe even get defensive. But if I ask "What do you hope to gain by doing that?" or "how does that action serve you?", you will likely revert to your emotions to find the answer. Of course, my tone of voice will be very important when asking the question. If I appear judgmental, you will answer with your intellect; if I am merely curious, you will look for a response within your feelings. Try asking yourself questions in a curious manner. For example, if you have made a mistake, instead of asking yourself "Why did I do that?" try asking "What was I hoping to accomplish?"and then "How might I better accomplish that?"or "What can I learn from what happened"?

In order to successfully reprogram the unconscious mind, we need to learn new patterns. Further, in order to learn new patterns, we must speak the language of the unconscious, which is thought mixed with strong emotion. Thought without emotion will keep you in the conscious mind. By mixing in feelings (the more intense the better), you advance into the unconscious, because it was the feelings you had about past events that created your programming.

> *"We do not learn; and what we call learning is only a process of recollection."*
> —*Plato*

So, if you focus on positive emotions, with intense feeling, you will be well on your way to reprogramming your unconscious mind. Remember, you cannot forever banish negative thoughts; you either just let them slip away by giving them no energy, or convert them to positive thoughts through reframing. We will go into reframing, or changing the context of something to give it new meaning, in the chapter *Talk to Yourself*.

> *"The more intensely we feel about an idea or a goal,*
> *the more assuredly the idea, buried deep in our subconscious,*
> *will direct us along the path to its fulfillment."*
> —Earl Nightingale

The average person has between 40,000 and 60,000 conscious thoughts per day, and people believe 99% of what they think. Your thoughts drift into your unconscious and become your beliefs, and beliefs become your destiny. The key is not to believe everything you think. I know…sounds easy, but what about nagging thoughts that just won't go away?

Remember…a thought is just a thought. When you fixate on a thought, you are giving it energy, and making it more real to you. If you get upset with yourself for thinking negative thoughts, you are involving your emotions as you think of the negative thought, further imbedding the programming. Allow your thoughts. Do not judge them.

> *"Basically we are all the same human beings with the same potential*
> *to be a good human being or a bad human being … The important*
> *thing is to realize the positive side and try to increase that; realize*
> *the negative side and try to reduce. That's the way."*
> —Dalai Lama

Imagine you are at a busy train station, with many trains speeding by and you get to choose on which one you will board. Your mind is that train station, and every train represents a thought. Thoughts will pop into your head, but you get to choose which train of thought on which to go for a ride. As a negative thought goes by, choose not to get on that train. Do not judge it as a bad train, just not the one you are choosing right now. Instead look for the train that will get you to your chosen destination, and climb on that train.

It is important to understand that if you get on the wrong train, accept it and move forward. Don't try to control your thoughts, just accept them and guide them in the direction you choose. Not every thought can be perfect or brilliant, and mistakes are often the best teachers. Take everything in stride, knowing it is just another part of your experience. Most importantly, remember if you try to get rid of negative thoughts, you are focusing on them...which gives them more power. So just gently get on a different train.

I was out for a drive the other day and was cut off by another driver, and as I slowed to let the driver merge (I no longer make other people's behavior my responsibility), I saw the driver talking on her cell phone. I started to think, *how rude, what a jerk, where are the cops now, oh yea, pulling someone over for not wearing a seatbelt, I should have been a cop, I'd love to sit there and wait for cell phone talkers*...and then I realized that I had leapt on the wrong train of thought...so I immediately switched trains and thought...*what a beautiful day, look at how many courteous drivers there are, I'll bet there was an emergency she had to get to and that's why she was on her phone, good thing I let her in, I need to stay safe on the road, when I get to where I'm going something good will be there, something good is there, I'm picking up my daughter, what a wonderful day.* My new train of thought allowed me to feel gratitude for all the wonderful things in my world.

Which way of thinking makes you feel better? Dwelling on something that is negative, irritating, or depressing, or allowing thoughts that make you feel happy, lucky and content?

> *"Every man has a train of thought on which he travels when*
> *he is alone. The dignity and nobility of his life, as well as his*
> *happiness, depend upon the direction in which that train is going,*
> *the baggage it carries and the scenery through which it travels."*
> —Joseph Fort Newton

Another way to control unwanted thoughts is to deliberately try to make the thought happen. Use any thought which creates worry or anxiety for you. Go ahead, do it now. You have the thought...good. Okay...now forget the thought and continue reading. Next, at various times during the coming week, deliberately try to take up that thought. When you get it, turn it off and think of something else. Your brain will become used to the idea that you have an on/off control.

Here is another technique: When you access a thought which is not helpful, visualize it in front of you, in black and white. Next, move it away from you, so that it becomes a mere speck. White out the speck. Now, think of a good thought, one you want, and move it closer, in living color. Move it very close so you can feel, taste, and smell it. Feel how good that thought feels. Go ahead...enjoy it.

What you are doing is training your brain to forget what isn't important or helpful, and to remember what is beneficial. You are using your conscious mind to reprogram your unconscious mind. You are consciously choosing the path for your unconscious.

> *"We must realize that the subconscious mind is the law of action and always expresses what the conscious mind has impressed on it. What we regularly entertain in our mind creates a conception of self. What we conceive ourselves to be, we become."*
> —Grace Speare

Why is it so hard to break or change habits? Neuroscience explains that information in your brain travels on neuro pathways. This intricate and complex information highway allows you to think about what you are reading, while your mind wanders to whatever thought was triggered by the reading material. Your mind is capable of bouncing back and forth between the written material and your triggered thoughts, over and over again. This complex system not only allows your experience of pleasure, but also helps you survive. Anything you ever remembered has created a pathway. The first time you burned your hand, a pathway was formed to prevent a repeat of that behavior. In fact, any experience of pain or pleasure, physical or emotional, prompts your brain to determine a cause, record it in your nervous system, and create a pathway, or "pattern".

When you perform an act for the first time, you create a connection, a thin, neural strand which allows you to re-access that behavior. Each time you repeat the behavior, you add another strand. Repeat it enough times, and the strands combine to form a powerful cable. In the gym, cables that hold hundreds of pounds of weight are merely a combination of many fine strands of wire, which individually would not hold much weight at all. It is the repetition of the wires which creates the strength. The more you engage in any pattern of behavior, the stronger the pathway becomes, just as if you were adding another strand to the cable.

The power of this pathway is why will power, or simply deciding to change on a conscious level, is usually ineffective. Your neuro associations are survival tools and are locked in your nervous system. That is why, for example, a person who no longer wants to smoke will continue to smoke, or an overweight person will continue to eat excessively, or an angry person continues to lose his temper. The good news is that when you stop indulging in the unwanted behavior long enough and thereby interrupt your pattern, the neural connection will weaken, in the same way that your muscles weaken and atrophy when they are no longer used. Interrupting a pattern is the start, but relating intense pain to the unwanted behavior and intense pleasure to the desired behavior is the most powerful tool in making the change. This is because it was pain or pleasure, either real or imagined, which contributed to the neuro association being formed in the first place.

Sometimes the brain will receive mixed messages, like associating pleasure with both the old, unwanted behavior and the new changed action. You may even associate pain with both...or both pain and pleasure with both behaviors. No wonder sustainable change is so difficult. Yo-yo dieting and recurrent smoking are some examples. The neural pathway may say "I am in so much pain from being fat, but that jelly donut would taste so good." "I am in pain from being bored, and taking that drug would allow me to escape." For lasting change, you first have to decide, clearly, what you want. Not what you don't want, but what you do want.

The next thing is to decide you want the change now. Not later, when you have hit bottom and the pain is too great, and you are out of excuses. Picture hitting bottom and use that as a resource. When you associate intense emotional pain with the old behavior, and all you can link with the new behavior is intense pleasure, the neuro pathways will begin to change. Every time you link intense pain to the old behavior and pleasure to the new one, you are adding another strand to the cable, and weakening a strand on the old one.

> *"The secret of success is learning how to use pain and pleasure instead of having pain and pleasure use you. If you do that, you're in control of your life. If you don't, life controls you."*
> —Tony Robbins

～～～

Altering the images in your mind to create a new meaning can be as simple as the following story I heard at an NLP seminar.

A lady with obsessive compulsive disorder (OCD) had been in therapy for years but just couldn't stop vacuuming the carpet in her house. All day long, over and over again, she would vacuum the floor. The NLP practitioner asked her the reasons for vacuuming. She answered *"all the footprints, I have to clean up all of the footprints."* He asked *"Where do the footprints come from?"* She said *"My family, they just keep making footprints."* He asked *"What would it mean if there were no footprints?"* He saw the color drain out of her face as she sat there for a minute and then quietly said *"I'd be alone."* Needless to say, she was cured of this obsession. A simple reframe of the footprint meaning caused her internal representations to change, thereby changing her life. What happened was that the pictures in her mind changed, both in quality, distance, clarity, and importance... and subsequently their meaning changed.

～～～

Milton Erickson was a legendary hypnotist and therapist who got clinical hypnosis approved by the AMA in 1957. His work was also one of the primary influences behind the science of Neuro-Linguistic Programming (NLP). He lived a life of accomplishment and achievement. He was widely admired and respected when he died in 1980. His story is an example of the power of the human spirit and the power of mind training, even when faced with insurmountable adversity.

Erickson struggled with polio since the age of 17. He was so severely paralyzed, his doctors were convinced he would die. Here is how Erickson recalled one night...

"As I lay in bed that night, I overheard the three doctors tell my parents in the other room that their boy would be dead in the morning. I felt intense anger that anyone should tell a mother her boy would be dead by morning. My mother then came in with as serene a face as can be. I asked her to arrange the dresser, push it up

against the side of the bed at an angle. She did not understand why, she thought I was delirious. My speech was difficult. But at that angle by virtue of the mirror on the dresser I could see through the doorway, through the west window of the other room. I was damned if I would die without seeing one more sunset. If I had any skill in drawing, I could still sketch that sunset."

Erickson survived that horrible night, of course, but for a while he was almost completely incapacitated in bed and unable to speak. Most amazingly, he did not give up and wallow in despair and self pity. Again, here are Erickson's own words...

"I had polio, and I was totally paralyzed, and the inflammation was so great that I had a sensory paralysis too. I could move my eyes and my hearing was undisturbed. I got very lonesome lying in bed, unable to move anything except my eyeballs. I was quarantined on the farm with seven sisters, one brother, two parents, and a practical nurse. And how could I entertain myself? I started watching people and my environment. I soon learned that my sisters could say "no" when they meant "yes." And they could say "yes" and meant "no". They could offer another sister an apple and hold it back. And I began studying nonverbal language and body language. I had a baby sister who had begun to learn to crawl. I would have to learn to stand up and walk. And you can imagine the intensity with which I watched as my baby sister grew from crawling to learning how to stand up."

Erickson did eventually walk again, by watching his baby sister. Then he faced another challenge...how to make his own way in the world and earn a living. His family were farmers and he had intended to follow in his father's footsteps but he was too weak from the polio to do that. Instead he wondered if he could become a doctor and so, off he went to medical school. Erickson turned out to be a gifted student and obtained a psychology degree while he was studying medicine. He went on to enjoy great success in his chosen field, but further challenges lay ahead. In his fifties Erickson developed post-polio syndrome, characterized by pain and muscle weakness caused by chronic over-use of partially paralyzed muscles. The condition worsened his paralysis. However, having been through the experience once before, he now had a strategy for recovering the use of his muscles. After this second recovery, he was confined to a wheelchair and suffered chronic pain, which he controlled with self-hypnosis...

"It usually takes me an hour after I awaken to get all the pain out. It used to be easier when I was younger. I have more muscle and joint difficulties now... Recently the only way I could get control over the pain was by sitting in bed, pulling a chair close, and pressing my larynx against the back of the chair. That was very uncomfortable: But it was discomfort I was deliberately creating."

Imagine that...pressing his larynx against the back of the chair to create discomfort in an attempt to control his pain. Despite all these challenges he lived life to the fullest.

His professional achievements were extraordinary and he left a lasting legacy to the worlds of psychology, psychiatry, psychotherapy, and communication. Who would have imagined that all this lay ahead of Erickson back on that night when he was 17 and nobody expected him to survive another day?

Well, perhaps Erickson himself did. You see, incredibly, Erickson regarded his terrible illness as an advantage! He said... *"We learn so much at a conscious level and then we forget what we learn and use the skill. You see I had a terrific advantage over others. I had polio and I was totally paralyzed."*

Erickson turned what most people would regard as a fatal blow into the foundation and inspiration for his own recovery. He also caused an incredible advance in human knowledge of benefit to millions of people.

So how will you react as you face your own challenges? Do you believe me when I say... "It's not what happens to you that matters, what matters is what you do about it."

When you find it hard to keep these words of wisdom in mind and act on them, think of the story of Milton Erickson. Perhaps the most valuable thing he left us was his example; the power of the human spirit and mind in overcoming adversity.

> *"Every adversity, every failure, every heartache carries with it the seed of an equal or greater benefit."*
> —Napoleon Hill

4.2 WHAT ARE YOU THINKING ABOUT?

*"You become what you think about all day long and
those days eventually become your lifetime."*
—Wayne Dyer

Now that you have learned about your unconscious mind, let's work a little on your conscious thoughts, and on how they tie together. Have you heard about the "law of attraction" which states that whatever you believe, you get to be right about and experience? Another way to say this is…life is a self fulfilling prophecy.

*"You are the masterpiece of your own life; you are the
Michelangelo of your experience. The David that you are
sculpting is you. And you do it with your thoughts."*
—Dr. Joe Vitale

Everything you do and everything you think about is a product of your core energy and mental habits. From what you think about when you wake up, to what you are thinking as you go to work, to what you think at leisure; you are a creature of mental habits. These habits can be very useful, as they allow us to accomplish intentions without even thinking about them. The drawbacks come when we do not like the results of our thoughts. As you become the awareness behind the thoughts, you can choose new thoughts and create new habits, habits that serve you better.

Are you afraid? Then whatever you fear will be drawn to you. Fear does have a purpose when it instructs you to gather more information before proceeding. Once you have attained whatever valuable information and insight you need…plunge ahead. Don't fall into the trap of paralysis by analysis. Most regrets come from what you didn't do.

Fear is how it feels to be confused and unaware. Except for rare instances of real danger, all fear is fear of the unknown. Fear also promotes further confusion, just like ignorance does… which is scary and generates more anxiety. Consequently, people routinely suffer from a vicious cycle of fear and ignorance, each feeding the other. Are you held back by the concern "what if something goes wrong"?

Fear... whether it is called anxiety, stress, tension, pressure, apprehension, nervousness, anger, guilt, worry or doubt... is not to be avoided, but rather embraced and overcome... get the necessary information on how to proceed...and then release the fear. Do not confuse cautiousness with fear. Releasing fear and stepping boldly forward is the mark of courage and true strength.

> *"Courage is not the absence of fear, but simply the mastery of fear."*
> —Mark Twain

Relax and ask yourself what is holding you back from your next dream. Listen carefully to see if it is the fear talking. Then ask yourself if the concerns are really deal breakers or just some scary noises in the background. If they are just scary noises, turn them off.

If you are in a dangerous situation, outpace your anxiety by focusing on what you want to do. If you don't focus on what you want, you are in your reactive mind (unconscious) instead of your thinking mind (conscious). When you start focusing on where you are heading, suddenly you are there.

> *"If you look into your own heart, and you find nothing wrong there, what is there to worry about? What is there to fear?"*
> —Confucius

All negative emotions are an offspring of fear. Fear is a lack of confidence in our future. Not wanting to feel helpless from the panic, we cover it up with other behaviors. More often than not, we are unconsciously attempting to hide fear from ourselves. We may channel our concern into worry or even depression. We may fear our lack of control over the way things are and convert the fear into anger against this perceived enemy (our lack of control and lack of faith). Below we will talk about some of the negative emotions that come from fear. If you see any of these in yourself, look inside and ask from where these feelings have come.

Fear can cause arrogance, which is usually controlled anger. We become arrogant when we unconsciously judge ourselves unworthy, and feel the need to construct a bold front to hide our insecurity. Next time you are dealing with an arrogant person, react with compassion, recognizing the force behind the arrogance. If you find yourself being arrogant, learn from it, forgive yourself, correct it, and let it go. When fear causes anger it attracts other angry people with whom to fight. You'll be pushing people back before they even push you. Fear causes you to act towards others as if they have violated your rights. Then, when your anger meets the anger of another, watch out. Remember, there is only one person who can cause you to be angry, and that person is looking back at you in the mirror. Deal with that person and get to the bottom of the anger's origin. (and read again the chapter on anger -*Understanding Anger)*.

Do you worry? Do you bring the imagined problems of tomorrow into today? Do you allow tomorrow's forecasted tragedy to cast its shadow backwards and lessen today's joy? Realize that your mind is not designed to project into the future, so it will just create imagined scenarios. Do you realize that if you think about something with enough emotion, you will create it? Are you creating the result of the worry? *"I knew that was going to happen"* are often the words of a worrier. Instead, think about your desired outcome. Albert Einstein said: *"you don't get what you want, you get what you expect"*.

> *"There is no point worrying because if something*
> *does happen, then you've lived it twice."*
> —Michael J. Fox

> *"Don't worry about the future...or worry, but know that worry is as*
> *effective as trying to solve an algebra problem by chewing bubble gum."*
> —The Big Kahuna (the movie)

Do you ever feel guilty?
You don't owe anyone anything and no one owes you.

> *"Friends don't owe friends. They do because they want to do."*
> —Rocky Balboa

It is a wonderful thing to give to others, but only when and where you choose...with no strings attached. Do not guilt yourself into actions, and do not use guilt to try to get someone else to do what you want. It is a toxicity that is in direct contrast with emotional fitness. If you are feeling remorse for a mistake you made in the past, see what you can learn from it and then forgive yourself and forge ahead.

"It is not how much we do, but how much love we put into doing it. It is not how much we give, but how much love we put into giving."
—Mother Teresa

Self consciousness is a fear of not being good enough. Most people feel this in one way or another. They are walking around thinking everyone is looking at them, and noticing all their shortcomings. Some self consciousness comes from childhood when your parents, in their effort to keep you safe, may have said things like: "No! Don't do that! You might get hurt! You don't know how! You are too little! When you were a child, the purpose of these messages was to keep you protected. Now that you are an adult, leave those feelings of inadequacy behind you. The best way to surpass these feelings is to forgive your parents for any errors they made; they were doing the best they could. And while you're at it …go ahead and pardon yourself for any mistakes you made.

Does forgiveness come easy for you? Forgiveness is letting go of fear. Can you be aware of other people's limitations without judging or condemning them? If someone remains negative, do you have the wisdom to forgive them and walk away? Forgiveness is essential to your emotional fitness. Forgiving does not mean condoning what someone did or even letting them back into your life. It simply means letting go of the negative energetic connection.

"Forgiving others is a gift to yourself, given not because the other deserves pardon, but because you deserve the serenity and joy that comes from releasing resentment and anger, and from embracing universal forgiveness."
—Jonathan Lockwood Huie

"Forgiveness is unlocking the door to set someone free and… realizing that you were the prisoner."
—Max Lucado

"The weak can never forgive. Forgiveness is the attribute of the strong."
—Mahatma Gandhi

Are you sad? Sadness is a natural response to significant loss, and helps you understand your values. Feeling and expressing sorrow is healthy, but eventually you must allow release and move towards acceptance. Accept what is and find an opportunity to learn; to grow wiser, kinder, and stronger. Think about what it means to be sad for no good reason. Do you focus on everything that is missing from your life? All that you do not have? How unfair it all is? If these are your thoughts, try instead focusing on all the abundance in your life. Stop comparing yourself to people who have more, and try looking at those with less. Self pity is very toxic behavior.

> "Self pity is our worst enemy and if we yield to it,
> we can never do anything wise in this world."
> —Helen Keller

> "Develop an attitude of gratitude, and give thanks for everything
> that happens to you, knowing that every step forward is a step toward
> achieving something bigger and better than your current situation."
> —Brian Tracy

Do you have gratitude? That is a good choice of where to put your thoughts. Now add a huge dose of love and optimism. No love in your life? No problem; when you start focusing your thoughts on love, optimism and gratitude, love in your life will materialize. Moreover, angry people will virtually disappear. What if something "Bad" happens? Don't worry; nothing means anything until you give it meaning. You can interpret an event as horrible and choose to feel like a victim, or you can interpret that same event as an opportunity to learn something valuable. Negative emotions cannot exist when you are in a state of gratitude. Try stepping into a state of joy and gratitude right now. If it feels good, make a habit to do it at least three times per day, even if it is just for 5 or 10 seconds. Enjoy your creation of a neuro pathway to joy.

> "He is a wise man who does not grieve for the things
> which he has not, but rejoices for those which he has."
> —Epictetus

How about responsibility? When you hold yourself responsible, you have a lot more influence over the outcome. What do you want? Take responsibility to decide how you are going to achieve it and what it will feel like at the finish line. Then make it happen!

> *"Having a vision for what you want is not enough!*
> *Vision without execution is hallucination."*
> —Thomas Edison

You cannot always control what pops into your head, but you certainly have a choice about which thoughts to dwell on and make important. Your thoughts are powerful because they create emotions. If you carry a negative or disempowering thought as just a thought without allowing it to become a feeling, you can just laugh about it, as it will have no power. Let positive thoughts create your emotions.

Start forming these habits today. Each night as you are ready for sleep, think of everything that went right, and then release the day. Make a wish and drift off to sleep imagining that the wish is your reality right now. Greet the morning with joy and gratitude that you have been given another day when others, perhaps more worthy, were not...and choose to be happy throughout the day.

The Indian saint, Vivekananda, who lived over 100 years ago, explained it beautifully...

> *"All the powers in the universe are already ours.*
> *It is we who have out our hands before our eyes*
> *And cry that it is dark.*
>
> *We are what our thoughts have made us;*
> *So take care about what you think.*
> *Words are secondary*
> *Thoughts live; they travel far*
>
> *When an idea exclusively occupies the mind,*
> *It is transformed into an actual mental or physical state*
> *We reap what we sow*
> *We are the makers of our own fate*
> *No one else has the blame, no one else has the praise*
>
> *There is no help for you outside of yourself,*
> *You are the creator of the universe.*
> *Like the silkworm you have built a cocoon around yourself...*
> *Burst the cocoon and come out as the beautiful butterfly,*
> *As the free soul.*

Then alone, you will see the truth.
In one word, this ideal is that you are divine,
God sits in the temple of every human body."
—Swami Vivekananda (1863-1902*)*

There is an exercise from the ancient Tao tradition called the Inner Smile, which begins with feeling and visualizing a joyful image in our mind, then moving that smiling energy into our brain, our heart, our internal organs, and our spine, thanking each part of our body for its particular function as we continue. This process creates an appreciation and gratitude for our marvelous human body. It also improves our self esteem by consciously reprogramming to love ourselves inwardly and outwardly. By doing so, we attract positive people and desirable situations into our lives. This process is simple, yet the results are profound.

"Sometimes your joy is the source of your smile,
but sometimes your smile can be the source of your joy."
—Thich Nhat Hanh

4.3 TALK TO YOURSELF

"What you think about, you talk about.
What you talk about, you bring about."
—Dan Ellis

When someone says, "You should" most people's typical response is "Why should I?"or "I don't want to." This response can even occur when we already want to do something! The trick is to bring your "should" and your "want" in harmony because "wants" are typically much more effective at motivating you than "shoulds". Even when you obey a "should", the "I don't want to" response may still arise, waiting to emerge into a behavior.

So...the next time you are about to tell yourself that you should do something, pause . . . think about which aspects of the behavior would be enjoyable or pleasurable. Then, think about what you could say to yourself and how you could deliver this message to elicit a response of desiring, choosing, or wanting the behavior.

"Maturity is doing what you want to do,
even when your mother thinks it's a good idea."
—Paul Watzlawick

Take it a step further. Instead of wanting...allow. Instead of wanting to go to sleep tonight, allow yourself to go to sleep. Instead of wanting to improve your diet, allow yourself to enjoy better eating habits. Do you want love? Try allowing love to come into your life. After you choose what you desire... allow it.

"Happiness is a butterfly, which, when pursued, is always just beyond
your grasp, but which, if you sit down quietly, might alight on you."
—Nathaniel Hawthorne

Do you "need" to do something? Try-"It is important to me". What about when you "have to" or "must"? Try "desire to" or "choose to". Leave "try to" behind and opt for "intend to" or "aim to" instead. Often the first step in resolving an issue is talking and thinking about it so as to allow it to become a little smaller and less overwhelming. The key is to change the details, like "that issue" instead of "this problem". By doing so, you are able to "get some distance" on the conflict, and "get a better grip" on a solution.

You cannot get a "good hold" on something that is too big, too close, or looming over you. It is amazing how often the solution to a problem or difficulty becomes easier when you shift it a little further away through your use of language, and thereby adjust your mental picture. Our brains create a model of the outside world and then places ideas in that model as if they were things. Consciously changing the words we use to describe a "problem" changes the meaning to something more manageable in our mind.

What questions are you asking yourself? Our questions determine our thoughts. The quality of the questions asked causes the differentiation between happiness/success and misery/failure.

Remember that your brain, like a genie in a bottle, gives you the answers to whatever questions you ask...so consciously choose the formation of your questions. Then, after asking the right questions, the next step is to take action.

> *"Wherever you go, go with all your heart."*
> —Confucius

Do you tell yourself what not to do? "I won't be stressed" or "I won't get angry" is much more helpful when stated in a positive manner. Your unconscious mind does not see the negative, so if you focus on what you do not want...that is what your brain will retain.

> *"Be careful how you talk to yourself...because you are listening."*
> —Jeff Adams

If you are angry, change the word to disenchanted. Are you stressed about an upcoming challenge? Adjust the word to excited. Are you worried? Switch to concern, you will feel better being concerned than worried. If your trouble is with accomplishing a particular task, try saying, "this used to be a challenge for me and I am glad to be on the path to overcoming it". "My back is killing me" is not the kind of instruction you should be sending to yourself. Revise instead to "I am feeling my back progressing through its healing process".

Feeling depressed? Refine the feeling such that you are not on top of things now, but are happy to be on the road to a turn around. Do you feel overwhelmed? I prefer to see you as busy, challenged, or in demand. Feeling lonely? Looks to me like you are temporarily on your own... and available for whatever opportunity is around the next corner.

Instead of being furious, try feeling passionate, it's a better word to describe your intense feeling. Feeling impatient? I think you are anticipating and looking forward to something. Are you jealous because you are insecure about your partner? Try describing that feeling as over loving.

The methods we use to talk to ourselves have far reaching implications on all aspects of our lives. Have you ever failed? I think you were getting educated, learning, or maybe you just stumbled a little. Were you stupid? No...you were learning, or maybe just not being innovative.

Do you have a sinking feeling or are you underwater? Then swim over to the island of solutions. Is the weight of the world on your shoulders? Then put the world down and move on.

Your mindset controls your destiny. Have you hit a wall? Then enjoy the climb over it or the stroll around it or blast through it, whatever would be more fun for you. Is life tough? Try life is wonderful or life is a game. Or even...Life is a cabaret, old chum.

Even when you are feeling sick, simply realize your body is a self healing machine and it is in the process of cleansing. The way you talk to yourself will convert to your thoughts, and your thoughts will become...

4.4 POISON OR THE FOUNTAIN OF YOUTH...IT'S YOUR CHOICE

I was on a bike ride with a friend the other day. Along the bike path, there was some kind of walking event with a lot of people. These people did not understand bike path etiquette (if you are not familiar with bike path etiquette, it is the same as car etiquette, where you stay to the right). My friend was getting stressed by people stepping in front of us and walking on the wrong side of the path, totally oblivious to what was going on around them. As my friend chose to let this situation stress and frustrate her (yes...it was a choice) I chose to enjoy the ride, gliding around the people and stopping when necessary.

What do you think was the self talk that my friend chose? How did it compare to mine? Because of my friend's choice of thoughts, she experienced the feelings that accompanied those thoughts. Since those thoughts were negative, she released harmful chemicals into her body. Anytime you are stressed, unhappy, frustrated, mad, disappointed, angry, etc., you create draining, destructive energy. This, in turn, releases harmful chemicals into your body, like cortisol and adrenaline (these chemicals are harmful when they do not have an outlet, like fight or flight). The chemicals literally eat away at your cells and your life force, creating countless health and emotional problems.

As I was riding merrily along, enjoying this bike ride on a beautiful day, I was releasing good chemicals into my body (constructive, building, healing energy)...due to the thoughts that I chose to think, which resulted in feelings, which in turn resulted in my reality.

Here's another bike story: Recently I looked out to check on my bike, and I couldn't see it. In that split second, I thought it had been stolen, and my heart started pounding in my chest. As you know, the mind cannot tell the difference between a thought and reality. So my body reacted to the thought as if it were real. Once I realized that the bike was there, I was fortunate to be able to jump on my bike and burn off the adrenaline that was pumping through my system. When you are in a similar situation while in traffic, at the office, at home, or anywhere else, the chemicals that your body releases have nowhere to go. So they cause you harm and aging. Release enough of these harmful chemicals with your thoughts, and the result will be dis-ease.

> *"Drag your thoughts away from your troubles... by the ears,*
> *by the heels, or any other way you can manage it."*
> —Mark Twain

Your body is always striving for growth and survival. Sometimes it is striving for growth *or* survival. You may not realize how important growth is for your survival. Every day billions of cells in your body wear out and have to be replaced. To accomplish this, your body needs significant amounts of energy. In response to a threat, real or imagined, your body will turn off its growth mechanism in favor of its survival mechanism. It cannot do both efficiently at the same time. The longer you stay in the protection mode (stressed), the more you consume energy reserves which are needed for growth. As soon as you feel stress, your adrenal glands secrete "stress hormones". These immediately constrict the digestive tract and force life sustaining blood into your arms and legs, so you can fight off or run from the impending threat.

Before this stress happened, your blood was being supplied to your vital organs, and now, with a lack of blood to nourish them due to the stress, these vital organs are unable to engage in growth related functions.

The immune system also needs energy. Just think about your energy levels when your immune system is fighting off a cold or the flu. Well... when you are stressed, the energy that should be supplied to your immune system is being diverted to deal with this impending danger.

Did you know that stress hormones are so effective at suppressing the immune system that doctors sometimes give them to transplant recipients so their immune systems won't reject the foreign tissue?

When you release stress hormones, your ability to think clearly is compromised. These adrenal stress hormones suppress blood flow to your reasoning conscious mind, in favor of your subconscious mind's life sustaining reflexive actions. This makes sense from an evolutionary point of view. If you are walking down a path while you are fighting off an infection, and a lion jumps in front of you, all of your energy will go into the process that makes you run away, before you even know why. There will be no energy to fight the infection, because what good will it do to fight the infection if the lion eats you? Same with growth...no need for growth if you will not live to see tomorrow's sunrise, right? But in modern society, when you are stressed on a regular basis as if a lion is about to have you for lunch ...well...you get the point.

Examine your specific stressors. What is stressing you? Where did it come from? Is it real? Is it contributing any value at all to your life?

Thankfully, not all 50 trillion of your cells have to be in one mode or the other. You can survive while under stress, but, as you now know; chronic stress will compromise your vitality. Please understand that for true vitality and abundance, we need to not only avoid stress by responding the right way to a stressful situation, but we also need to actively seek out fulfilling, loving, and joyful lives, and thereby truly enjoy all the benefits of emotional fitness.

There is a growing body of research indicating that exercise improves immune function, helps lower blood pressure, boosts mood, and reduces stress and depression. Also, when we prescribe exercise as a medicine, there are no harmful side effects or downsides. In fact, a study from Oxford University supports a long held theory that good hard laughter triggers an increase in endorphins, the brain chemicals that make you feel good, distract you from pain, and deliver many other health benefits.

> *"What soap is to the body, laughter is to the soul."*
> —Yiddish Proverb

So...you have a choice...to release harmful chemicals into your body (poison), or to release good chemicals into your body (fountain of youth). Next time you decide to get stressed, unhappy, frustrated, disappointed, angry, etc., please do not blame any other person or situation...it is your choice. Always has been, always will be. I am not saying you *should* only engage in positive self talk...I truly believe that you *want* to. You will feel better, live longer, look better, and have better relationships. Try it...what have you got to lose.

Here are some suggestions for positive self talk, which are also called affirmations. An affirmation is really every thought you have, and the goal is to choose thoughts that cause movement towards ideas that you desire... where you see what you want to see. After reading these suggestions, you might want to write down a few of your own. Believe these statements as you say them; thought mixed with emotion will allow them into your unconscious:

- Every time I feel discouraged I close my eyes and visualize the future I want. Then I open my eyes and start to build it.
- The moment I decide where I want to go, the world will make room for me.
- I was born with potential, goodness and trust. I was born with ideals and dreams. I will turn them into what I want – today.
- My world is full of opportunities. Today I am going to look for two I never noticed until now.
- I am making progress if each mistake is a new one.
- I will stop chasing the wrong things and allow the right things to catch up to me.
- There are a lot of steps between where I am and where I want to be. The real task is – How can I make each step fun?
- Today I will refuse to spend any time worrying about what might happen, and spend that time on what I want to have happen.
- If I can conceive and believe, I can achieve.
- Looking for happiness and not finding it is just the world telling me that I need to get more in touch with my own inner resources.
- Life isn't about finding myself, it's about creating myself.
- Happiness doesn't depend upon who I am or what I have, it depends on what I choose to think.
- Beneath the surface there is good in everyone. Today I am going to have fun spotting the good in everyone I meet.
- Happiness is not the absence of problems: happiness is learning to enjoy the problems.

According to Gregg Braden, author of *Deep Truth* (as well as many other books), it is the heart that sends a signal to the brain to release the appropriate chemicals. The optimum frequency between our heart and our head is 0.10 hertz. When we access positive emotions in our heart, such as gratitude, appreciation, care, and compassion, we arrive at that frequency. In addition, our DHEA (the precursor to all hormones) levels increase 100% and our stress hormones such as cortisol decrease 23%, and all this happens in just three minutes. Mr. Braden, who is internationally renowned as a pioneer in bridging science and spirituality, states that the words gratitude, appreciation, care, and compassion have been scientifically documented as words that accomplish optimal DHEA levels. Holding these words close to your heart will do wonders for your health and emotional fitness. Make it a bedtime ritual.

> *"A wise man does not grieve for the things that he has not,*
> *but rejoices for those which he has."*
> —Epictetus

4.5 A WORD ABOUT HAPPINESS

Happiness, for most of humanity, is like the ocean tides. The ebb and flow of circumstances affect our level of happiness. Your happiness should never be determined by outer circumstances. Instead, it needs to be decided by your own core energy.

"It isn't what you have, or who you are, or where you are, or what you are doing that makes you happy or unhappy. It is what you think about."
—Dale Carnegie

The best way to be happy is to just step into being happy for this moment only. Forget about the future and forget about the past...just be happy for this breath only. Then, if you liked that, try the next breath, and the next breath (More on this in the chapter "A Gift for You").

"I believe that the purpose of life is to be happy. From the moment of birth, every human being wants happiness and does not want suffering. Neither social conditioning nor education nor ideology affects this. From the very core of our being, we simply desire contentment. I don't know whether the Universe, with its countless galaxies, stars and planets, has a deeper meaning or not, but at the very least, it is clear that we humans who live on this earth face the task of making a happy life for ourselves."
—The Dalai Lama

Being happy is not just a gift you give to yourself, it is also a gift that you give to others. The nicest thing that you can do for everyone around you is to be happy. When you are unhappy, who do you think about? Let me guess...yourself. How about when you are happy? We all owe it to our friends, loved ones and even our acquaintances to be happy. If you need proof of this, ask any child what it is like to have an unhappy parent, or ask any parent what it is like to have an unhappy child. While you are at it, ask any wife what it is like to have an unhappy husband or ask any husband what it is like to have an unhappy wife. How about unhappy co-workers... or unhappy people you pass on the street?

Everyone desires happiness, even those people whose attempts to achieve happiness may not be in line with your beliefs. You should not let anyone's misguided attempts at happiness affect your peace of mind. It is challenging enough that your happiness is usually determined by your own beliefs, thoughts, and behavior, but when you condition it upon other people's behavior, you cause yourself an insurmountable challenge.

We all know that happiness is contagious... and so is unhappiness. Quantum physics explains this in detail, referring to the interconnectedness of all beings.

In his book *"Happiness is a Choice"*, Barry Neil Kaufman says it this way:

> *"What each of us learns has the potential of becoming a message to all humankind...If just one of us changes our beliefs and teaches happiness and love, then, that attitude or information goes into the connective tissue of the community and enhances the aptitude for happiness for the entire group...There is no other single energy on the planet greater than the joy and well being emanating from one truly happy and loving person"*

Although I have made the case in this book that you are not responsible for anyone else's happiness, there is a way to help others on their own road...believe in them. I think if you did a study of people in prison, along with all the unhappy people throughout society... you would find a common denominator, that most didn't feel loved or felt that no one believed in them.

> *"There comes that mysterious meeting in life when someone acknowledges who we are and what we can be, igniting the circuits of our highest potential."*
> —Rusty Berkus

When I was 19 years old, I had low self esteem. I was a troubled troublemaker with a lot of anger, which I vented towards other people. I was at a place where I could have wound up dead or in jail. Then, my life was significantly influenced by one guy, about 24 years old, who was called "Big Ed" (Ed McCree). He was a bigger than life individual who took a bunch of us ne'er do wells under his wing and taught us how to build houses. Big Ed saw something in me, as well as others, that we did not see in ourselves. Or maybe it wasn't what he saw, but simply how he chose to treat people. In large part based on what I unconsciously perceived as his belief in me, I went on to become a sub-contractor within a year. I found contractors to give me work even with my lack of experience because I now believed in myself. It was that simple act of someone whom I respected believing in me when I did not believe in myself that took me from the wrong path to the right path. Although we all looked up to Big Ed, he never looked down on us.

> *"It is not the failure of others to appreciate your abilities that should trouble you, but rather your failure to appreciate theirs."*
> —Confucius

Start now with someone in your life that you care about or love. Stop trying to make them happy or trying to "fix" them in any way... just believe in them and demonstrate that in the way you treat them. Maybe, if you are lucky, you will get to be the "Big Ed" in someone's life.

> *"You can't row someone across the river without getting to the other side yourself."*
> —Zig Ziglar

4.6 HOW TO BE HAPPY

Start by asking yourself this simple question" "Do I want to be happy, or do I not want to be happy?" Of course you will answer that you want to be happy. But what if something happens that you think should not have, something that you label as wrong or bad? You need to realize that the sole element in your control is the interpretation you give to the life events in front of you. Choose now how you interact with reality. If you choose to complain about it, that is one option. If you choose to resist it, that is also your right. If instead you select acceptance and embrace your interaction with life, you will have the power to choose happiness.

Sometimes events cause you to experience sadness and grief. Sadness is part of the human experience. When you understand that sadness is something you are experiencing and not something that you are, you maintain an inner sense of calm that allows you to weather any storm... and come out on the other side not only okay...but wiser, stronger, and better off from the experience. Billions of things will occur over which you have no control. The question remains, will you be happy regardless of what happens? You just need to let go of the part of yourself that wants to create melodrama. This part thinks there are good reasons to not be happy. You gain nothing by being bothered by the events of life, and there will always be something to bother you if you choose. Your resistance does not change the world, you just suffer. You were not put on earth to suffer. You are not helping anything by being miserable. Life is a game. If you stay happy...you win!

> *"If you're not happy all the time, it's because*
> *you messed it up inside your head"*
> —Michael Singer

There are three ways to alter the way you feel. The most important way is your perceptions, which we have discussed at length. But equally as powerful is your body physiology and your state of mind.

Imagine a depressed person walking into the room where you are now. What is their body physiology like? What I mean by that is... How is their posture? How is their breathing? How are they moving? What is the expression on their face? Now picture a happy person and ask the same questions. There...you know how to do depressed and you know how to do happy.

Get into a powerful body physiology and your thoughts will also be powerful. Dana Carney Ph.D and grad student Andy Yap of Columbia University along with Amy Cuddy of the Harvard Business School had 42 people assume either a power pose or a wimpy pose. After 2 minutes of posing, the power posture patients experienced widespread feelings of being in charge. But they took it a step further and swabbed saliva to gauge hormone levels. After a mere 2 minutes of posing, the people who assumed the take charge positions had more testosterone and less cortisol (stress hormone), whereas the opposite held true for the wimpy posers. The conclusion is that your body posture has a measurable effect at a molecular level, and every emotion you feel, or state you are in, has a specific physiology linked to it.

"If you say, 'I absolutely will do that,' and your physiology is unified — that is, your posture, your facial expression, your breathing pattern, the quality of your gestures and movements, and your words and tonality match — you absolutely will do it. Congruent states are what we all want to move toward, and the biggest step you can take is to be sure you're in a firm, decisive, congruent physiology. If your words and your body don't match up, you' re not going to be totally effective."
—Tony Robbins

Our emotions are nothing more than biochemical reactions in our brains. They can be sparked in an instant, which creates a state of mind. Become conscious of your emotional states and take control of them instead of living in a reactive way.

You have over 80 muscles in your face, so if you have been doing sad or depressed for awhile, you may have habitual muscle patterns that are dictating your states. Start to feel good, smile, breath deeply, and laugh. Keep it up to retrain your body physiology to naturally default to a positive state.

Is the body physiology the cause of the state of mind or the state of mind the cause of the body physiology? It is an endless cycle, with each feeding off the other. Try focusing on good thoughts to trigger your physiology and focus on your physiology to trigger good thoughts. Direct your thoughts to your goals and be sure your physiology is in harmony with those thoughts.

Avoid fearful, worried, frustrated, depressed and any other negative states. If you find yourself in a negative state, immediately change your physiology to create empowered, motivated, excited, enthusiastic, creative, and happy states.

When someone is experiencing stress, anxiety, sadness, guilt or worry…it's rarely about "why" and more about "how." "Why" is just the story they've been telling themselves for so long that they are convinced is true. If you are sad, how are you doing sad? How would you do happy? What would your posture be like, your facial expressions, your thoughts, your breathing?

> *"Thus the sovereign voluntary path to cheerfulness, if our spontaneous cheerfulness be lost, is to sit up cheerfully, to look around cheerfully, and to act and speak as if cheerfulness were already there."*
> —William James

Your best chance of happiness is when you realize that you are doing what you choose to do. However, you may have to accomplish tasks you do not particularly like because they are serving the mission you have chosen. If you are not happy performing these tasks or with the mission you have chosen, choose a new mission. I have met very successful people who are not happy and feel they are stuck in the life they created. If they realized they could change their priorities at any time, they would relinquish complaints. They just have to change the way they perceive themselves and the world around them.

> *"If you don't like the road you're on…*
> *Start paving another one"*
> —Luke Dawson

———

Before ending this chapter, I would like to remind you of something you have learned throughout this book. *Your happiness will be determined by the questions you choose to ask yourself.* If something horrible is occurring, ask yourself "what can I learn from this?" or "how important will this be in ten years?" or "how can I use this situation for the greater good?" Asking these types of questions will immediately change your focus. Then, once you have successfully changed your focus, decide to change your body physiology to one that reflects the state of mind you have chosen.

I have a few questions to ask you right now…What are a few pleasant things that have presented themselves so far today? What are you pleased about in your life right now? If circumstances are so awful that you say that you have nothing to be happy for, ask yourself… "What could I be happy about right now if I really wanted to be?" Then go on to ask yourself… "To what or whom am I grateful?" This is a very empowering question because you cannot experience gratitude and a negative emotion at the same time.

"Make up your mind that you will be happy whether you are rich or poor, healthy or unhealthy, happily married or unhappily married, young or old, smiling or crying. Don't wait for yourself, your family, or your surroundings to change before you can be happy within yourself. Make up your mind to be happy within yourself, right now, whatever your are, or wherever you are."
—Paramahansa Yogananda

4.7 LIFE IS TOUGH

When life throws you the toughest challenges, your opportunity for growth is the greatest. If you were to help a caterpillar during his struggle in the cocoon, he would never have the strength to develop into a beautiful butterfly. When a fish spends its life in a tank, being fed regularly, it doesn't grow as strong as it would if fending for itself. It is only through strain that a muscle will develop. Irritate an oyster enough and it will produce a pearl. Put a lump of coal under enough pressure... you end up with a diamond.

*"One who gains strength by overcoming obstacles possesses
the only strength which can overcome adversity."*
—Albert Schweitzer

*"Stand up to your obstacles and do something about them. You will
find that they haven't half the strength you think they have."*
—Norman Vincent Peale

To develop substance as a human being, we must develop character, and character is best developed through experience, sometimes hard, bitter and difficult experience. Adversity is not something to be feared and avoided, but rather something to be welcomed, embraced, and overcome.

*"The world ain't all sunshine and rainbows. It is a very mean and nasty place.
It will beat you to your knees and keep you there permanently if you let it. You,
me or nobody is going to hit as hard as life. But it ain't about how hard you're
hit, it is about how hard you can get hit and keep moving forward, how much can
you take and keep moving forward. That's how winning is done! If you know
what you're worth, go out and get what you're worth. But you gotta be willing
to take the hits. And not pointing fingers saying you aren't where you wanna
be because of him or her or anybody. Cowards do that and that ain't you.
You're better than that."*
—Rocky Balboa

At a life coaching workshop I attended, we were discussing "victim to victor" and a man stood up to tell his story. His story was how he went from "miserable to miracle". About 6 years before, he was diagnosed with fibromyalgia, which is a condition that causes muscle pain, weakness, and severe fatigue, along with many other symptoms. He went into a deep depression and lost all will to lead a productive life. He lost so much during this period… too much to go into here. After several years of misery, he stumbled upon the teachings of life coaching. He said "Once I learned the tools and perspectives and way of being, it returned me to joy and seeing the gifts life brought me. Every minute of every day I know I have the tools to coach myself, and I don't have to rely on anyone else". He went on to say "We all have complete control of how we receive and embrace the gifts. Instead of being a victim, I am empowered". What can we learn from his motivational story? Change can come in an instant with a shift of perception. Happiness is easy and takes much less effort than misery or sadness. As soon as he learned how to perceive his world differently…his world was different. With a shift of perception, he went from "miserable to miracle". I believe that he simply started asking himself the right questions….therefore receiving the right answers.

I'm reminded of a poem By William Earnest Henley:

"Out of the night that covers me, black as the pit from pole to pole
I thank whatever Gods may be, for my unconquerable soul

In the fell clutch of circumstance, I have not winced nor cried aloud
Under the bludgeonings of chance, my head is bloody but unbowed

Beyond this place of wrath and tears, looms but the horror of the shade
And yet the menace of the years, finds and shall find me unafraid

It matters not how strait the gate, how charged with punishment the scroll
I am the master of my fate; I am the captain of my soul."

The name of this poem is "Invictus" which means unconquered. The essence of the message is that no matter what happens to you, you get to decide how you will respond. You decide what you will do tomorrow and the next day, and you choose your attitude. You select what your goals will be and whether you will continue to move forward or give up. You are the master of your own fate.

Let me tell you about William Ernest Henley who wrote this poem. He loved writing but his family could only afford a second-rate school. At 12, he contracted tuberculosis which weakened and crippled his limbs. At 18, one foot had to be amputated. In spite if this, he vigorously worked and studied so he could reach his dream of being an author and poet. At the age of 24, just as his career was beginning, doctors told him that his other foot would need to be amputated. To avoid amputation, he traveled to Edinburgh where he was hospitalized for nearly 2 years undergoing radical new treatments. It was during these many, painful months in the hospital that he wrote "Invictus," which is a bold statement of his determination to overcome both his physical handicaps and depression.

When he was finally released from the hospital, he found work as an editor of a little-read magazine. Despite his setbacks, he continued to work and, little by little, his writings became world renowned. He became chief editor of the "National Observer" and used his career as an opportunity to help many up-and-coming authors. His unconquerable spirit drove him forward, undeterred by setbacks or challenges, until he accomplished his dream.

You too, are the master of your fate. You can decide, right now, what you desire out of life. Like William Earnest Henley, you can overcome any challenges to achieve your dreams. Now is your chance to take control and steer your life in any direction that you choose. You decide ... it is up to you.

Sometimes you just need to shed the demands that you place on yourself...even the demands to be happy. Just put your life in perspective. When you feel like life, or someone, betrayed you, it may be time to step aside, get impersonal, and ask "what am I supposed to learn from this?" Move forward, even if you do not have the answers. I trust that you know the story of Helen Keller, who was a normal, healthy child until the age of 18 months when she got sick and became blind and deaf. Even with this adversity, she went on to be one of the 20th century's leading humanitarians. She is a perfect example of learning to accept what happens to you and catapulting forward. Your spirit is a natural instrument of healing.

"Character cannot be developed in ease and quiet.
Only through experience of trial and suffering can the soul be strengthened,
vision cleared, ambition inspired, and success achieved."
—Helen Keller

Open up and allow your life to happen. You never know when and where the next break will come…when the door will open and your life will be transformed. Believe in yourself and that you were given this gift of life for a purpose, and your struggles are simply the price that you must pay to achieve your personal greatness.

"Strength and growth come only through continuous effort and struggle."
—Napoleon Hill

Try this: When you say "Life is tough" imagine yourself surrounded by compassion and love. Take a deep breath and inhale slowly, see the healing white light of compassion and love enter into you and go through every cell of your body, nourishing each cell with healing white light. As you exhale, exhale out everything that you believe is causing you pain. Then inhale a deep breath of all that IS good in your life, and exhale out all that you feel is undesirable.

Trust in the process of life. Do not demand your life to be complete before you love and trust it. Just begin where you need to commence in that process. Where you need to start is right here and right now.

"Close your eyes…
Fall in love…
Stay there."
—Rumi

5. WHO'S CONTROLLING YOU?

The goal of this book is to help you master thinking in an emotionally fit way. To do this, you must take command of your thoughts, beliefs, and belief systems. There are always challenges. Modern medicine, politics, advertising, and organized religion may try to accomplish your thinking for you...to fulfill their desire to guide you. If you do not agree with everything I share with you here, that's okay. The goal is to have you think for yourself and make your own choices.

> *"The choices we make by accident are just as*
> *important as the choices we make by design."*
> —Dr. Shad Helmstetter

In my study of hypnosis, I experienced the awesome power of suggestion, even when not associated with hypnosis. A suggestion is a thought, idea, word, belief, command, proposition, plea or action dispensed in any manner, be it direct or indirect...conscious or unconscious...that will alter a person's normal behavior pattern. There are times when a person accepts a suggestion and acts upon it without the reflective or critical thoughts that should normally occur.

Direct suggestions are conveyed in an authoritative or persuasive manner, like when you see the flashing red lights in your rear view mirror and you pull over without consciously choosing to do so. Another example is when someone is being persuasive in seeking to sell you a product, idea, or belief.

Indirect or inferred suggestions are not recognized as suggestions because they are non-verbal, often only motions or sounds, when you smile and that causes others to smile, when you look up and watch others do the same. An inferred suggestion might be a signal for someone to "come here" or pointing to suggest they leave the room. It can be as straightforward as a nod of the head to indicate approval or disapproval, or a fist to threaten violence.

A prestige suggestion is accepted or acted upon without a "second thought" or question because it was given by a person of prestige, such as a doctor, lawyer, teacher, politician, parent, celebrity, author, etc.

Non-prestige suggestions are conditioned reflexes such as music or atmosphere prompting certain emotions such as happiness, sadness, dancing, singing, or romance. The sight or smell of certain foods might suggest hunger. Show me a picture of pizza and I immediately crave a slice. Similarly, certain noises might evoke excitement or stress. An example of an environmental suggestion is when a clear sunny day makes you feel full of vitality, or a dismal or rainy day makes you feel lethargic or sluggish. Fresh air or stuffy air, or too hot or too cold will influence how you feel and how happy you remain.

There is nothing inherently wrong with responding to suggestions. Emotional fitness is when you are aware of and consciously choose if and how you desire to respond.

"It is always wise to raise questions about the most obvious and simple assumptions."
—C. West Churchman

5.1 MODERN MEDICINE

I am not a medical professional and I make no medical or moral judgments about those who choose to receive chemical aid. The key word in the preceding statement is "choose". We have discussed the term "prestige suggestion". When you see certificates on the wall and the white lab coat on your doctor, you are more likely to accept and act upon their recommendations without a "second thought" because they were dispensed by a person of prestige. Be aware of the influence before you give up your power of choice.

"Don't cede control to the disease cartel."
—Dr. Walter Bortz, a Stanford University professor
and author of the book "Next Medicine".

Realize that when your doctor prescribes a drug for you, the drug is adjusting one or more components of the complex and intricate information pathways of your body. Even though the drug may have a positive effect, there is also the possibility of unwanted consequence. This is why pharmaceutical drugs come with information sheets listing not only the positive actions, but also the side effects that can range from irritating to deadly. It is important to understand the risks as well as the benefits before taking any drug, because when a drug is introduced to correct a specific dysfunction, it is also being delivered by the blood to the entire body.

"It is easy to get a thousand prescriptions but hard to get one single remedy."
—Chinese Proverb

So before you incorporate a drug into your life, remember to look at the side effects and make an informed decision. Remember that this "cure" might be worse than the disease and at times can result in the need for more medications to deal with the drug-induced side effects.

Medication Madness by Dr. Peter Breggin provides more than fifty cases where mood altering prescription drugs played a role in suicide, murder, and other violent and criminal behaviors.

"The doctor of the future will give no medicine but will interest his patients in the care of the human frame, in diet and in the cause and prevention of disease."
—Thomas Edison

It is not just serious issues like depression that can generate problems. In the December 2011 issue of Mens Health, there is an article about the baldness drug Propecia. Data has been available for some time that this drug produces "adverse sexual effects" in up to 15% of the men that take it. Even worse than the physical effect, evidence suggests that this particular drug can penetrate the brain and disrupt key chemicals therein, such as neurosteroids, which are brain chemicals that play a role in reducing anxiety, enhancing memory, regrowing brain cells, and helping us sleep.

In Mens Health June 2011, there is an article that recommends you avoid taking nonsteroidal anti-inflammatories (NSAIDs...like Advil, aspirin, etc.) after sundown, as these drugs can affect levels of sleep promoting agents in your brain. These drugs may delay your ability to fall asleep, and cause increased agitation during the night. In addition, in a Kaiser Permanente study, it was determined that men who took NSAID's were more likely to have erectile dysfunction (ED). If the problem is sore muscles...perhaps you should take a hot bath instead. If it's a headache, relax and unwind with some meditation or yoga.

"150 people die every year from being hit by falling coconuts.
Not to worry, drug makers are developing a vaccine."
—Jim Carrey

Did you know that taking acetaminophen (found in Tylenol and several other medicines) can lead to liver toxicity resulting in liver failure?

"Drugs are not always necessary. Belief in recovery always is."
—Norman Cousins

What about alternative medical options such as chiropractic that do not use drugs? In 1990, the American Medical Association was found liable in court for illegal attempts to discredit and destroy the chiropractic profession.

A friend of mine was experiencing horrible neck pain from degenerated discs in her neck. The pain was so bad that she was taking Advil every day. The medical specialist (orthopedic surgeon) informed her that her choices were either surgery or injections into her neck. The first time she received the injection, she attained relief for about three months. The second time, they missed the spot and she got a lump on the back of her neck at the injection site. She was in so much discomfort, she decided to try again, and secured a little relief for a few months. She then heard of laser therapy for similar conditions so she asked the doctor for his opinion and he said it didn't work and was quackery. He said her alternatives were to endure the pain or have surgery, which entailed cutting through the front of her neck to her spine and fusing the discs together. After many more months of suffering, she met Doctor David Barold, who was an MD offering an alternative option. After ten sessions of decompression and laser therapy, she experienced nothing short of a miracle. She became virtually pain free, and no longer even needed Advil. She could lean her head back and look up, movements she had not been capable of for many years.

The conclusion is...do not only listen to the first "expert" with whom you speak. Get more information elsewhere (from other "experts", books, journals, etc) and make your own decision. To be clear, I do not mean to discredit the valuable opinions of experts, but only I can make any final decision for myself.

Parents...please be careful if someone advises to put your highly active, enthusiastic child on drugs. Well meaning parents, who would not consider giving their 7 year old marijuana or any other street drug, will give them a prescription drug because of "Doctor's orders". Get the facts and then decide. There are definitely occasions where drugs can be the right choice for your child's behavioral problem, but it should never be a rash determination. Consider counseling or life coaching first, or perhaps even a change in diet. Starting a child on drugs should be adopted as a last resort, not as a quick fix for a complex concern.

For almost all health problems, from depression to obesity to high blood pressure, combining exercise with proper eating habits is the best choice. Sadly, we don't hear too much about exercise from the powerful pharmaceutical industry...because they have not yet figured out how to put it in a pill.

"He's the best physician that knows the worthlessness of the most medicines."
—Benjamin Franklin

"Change your beliefs, energy, and diet; and you will
change the way your gene's express themselves."
—Dr. Mathew James

Remember, your doctor is in business. The hospital is a business. The drug companies are a business. Businesses must sell their wares to stay in business.

"I got the bill for my surgery.
Now I know what those doctors were wearing masks for."
—James H. Boren

The point I want to make here is...take responsibility for your choices. They are yours and no one else's. Western medicine is excellent at treating injuries and diagnosis. Medical treatment, including surgery and prescription drugs can play an important role in keeping you well. Just please...get the facts and make your own decision. Emotional fitness is when you realize that every choice has a consequence, so you make selections that honor your personal needs and values.

"Health is a state of complete physical, mental and social well-being,
and not merely the absence of disease or infirmity."
—World Health Organization, 1948

5.2 POLITICS

"Politics is the art of looking for trouble, finding it whether it exists or not, diagnosing it incorrectly, and applying the wrong remedy."
—Earnest Benn

What is the purpose of wars between countries? Millions of people are killed and maimed, and for what? The horrors that humans inflict on each other are unspeakable. At one time, wars were about borders and boundaries. There would be a start date and an end date. Now… wars are about ideas and therefore, cannot be won.

"We are nuclear giants but when it comes to peace, we are infants."
—General Omar Bradley

This is a book about your emotional fitness. In life, if you do not like something, you have two options. Either work towards change, or accept the current situation. Too many people allow politics to upset them but never engage in any transforming behavior. This is the phenomenon of high emotional investment with low level of involvement, or caring too much and doing too little. Resistance alone only achieves stress and its resultant health problems, and will not improve or change anything for the better.

"The reason many people in our society are miserable, sick, and highly stressed is because of an unhealthy attachment to things they have no control over."
—Steve Maraboli

Some people become so emotionally involved with their political beliefs that it shapes their identity. They say "I am a Republican" or "I am a Democrat" rather than saying "I believe the philosophies of that party". It becomes an "I'm right and you're wrong" mentality. They are only interested in others possessing the same beliefs as they have, and do not want to hear another person's point of view.

"He who knows only his side of the case, knows little of that."
—John Stuart Mill

History shows us that every version of community eventually crumbles, and when it does, you as an individual are exposed. Understand how to manage yourself and create your own life plan that does not depend on the government. Whether you want to change yourself or change the world, you should realize that no one can do it for you. After all is said and done...it is all up to you.

"Independence of nation begins with independence of self."
—Jonathan Lockwood Huie

5.3 ADVERTISING

The mission of advertising is to influence you to take particular actions or to buy specific products. Advertisers try to manipulate you into associating happiness with their commodity. I have a friend whose visualization of heaven is to sit and relax on a beautiful beach, maybe in a hammock, maybe on a chair. Is it any wonder she loves Corona beer, whose advertisements paint the picture she relates to pleasure?

What advertising tries to achieve is a link of their products to your pleasure receptors, so you will want to experience the association. Why does McDonalds have a clown? That's right, to attract children. If they can link enough pleasure to their products, you will overlook the pain their merchandise may cause. Obesity in America is caused in part by advertisers linking so much pleasure to unhealthy processed foods. Similarly, people might buy designer clothes or objects because they associate them with the celebrity or lifestyle that advertises the product.

> *"Programmers and marketing people know how to get into your*
> *subconscious - they spend millions of dollars researching colors, shapes,*
> *designs, symbols, that affect your preferences, and they can make you*
> *feel warm, trusting, like buying. They can manipulate you."*
> —Richard Hatch

Embedded commands in advertising is also problematic. Look at this advertising message:

> "I need to tell you about the new book *The Truth in Advertising*. It has just hit the shelves. By now, you've probably heard there was a small delay to get it in the bookstores and on Amazon.com, but I'm pleased to announce that I can get it there now without any problems. I feel proud to have done it at last".

Innocent enough advertisement, right? If it were on the radio or TV, with some skill on the part of the orator, as far as the tone of voice and special gestures, your unconscious would hear:

> "I **need** to tell you about the **new book The Truth in Advertising.** It has just hit the shelves. **By now**, you've probably heard there was a small delay to **get it in the bookstores and on Amazon.com**, but I'm pleased to announce that I can **get it there now** without any problems. I **feel proud to have done it at last**".

Now, look at just the bold portion:

Need new book, The Truth in Advertising. Buy now. Get it in the bookstore and on Amazon.com. Get it there now. Feel proud to have done it at last.

Your conscious mind hears the entire message, but with delivery skill, your unconscious catches the embedded part. It is happening to you all the time. When you do not know why you want to buy something...you are probably being influenced unconsciously, possibly by advertising.

Flex your emotional fitness muscles. Link pleasure to making your own choices, and pain to being manipulated by others. Do this by being aware of what is motivating your choices. We are not driven by reality, rather by our interpretations and our perceptions of reality.

When you treat the information you are getting from various sources – the media, the government, your doctor, the church, advertising, experts, films and books, even this book...with just a little skepticism, you get to choose whether or not you wish to believe the message or not.

If you decide that a message is one that is good for you, by all means sit back, relax and enjoy the message for all it is worth. But if you conclude that this is not something that you want in your life, just simply look at it and say *"Hey, that's not how I choose for my reality to work"*. Your end result will be acceptance of only beliefs that you really do want. Since your beliefs become your reality, you create your own world...your own choice... and that's what you really want, isn't it?

> *"The strongest principle of growth lies in the human choice."*
> —George Eliot

5.4 ORGANIZED RELIGION

I enjoy and appreciate the ancient teachings of great philosophers and masters including Lau Tzu, Gandhi, Buddha, and Jesus Christ. I believe these men were rare and special human beings. They did not position themselves as divine beings, and certainly not as the initiators of all the trappings that have followed after them. I believe that their role, as well as the role of countless other spiritual leaders, was to model the highest potential of the human spirit and to inspire people to understand the spiritual purpose within the human experience.

For me, spirituality means being in touch with the part of yourself that is seeking meaning and purpose. It is the light inside of you that is drawn to hope and will not give in to despair.

> *"I believe in God, but not as one thing, not as an old man in the sky. I believe that what people call God is something in all of us. I believe that what Jesus and Mohammed and Buddha and all the rest said was right. It's just that the translations have gone wrong."*
> —John Lennon

Separating one group of people from another is the polar opposite of spirituality. When organized religious activity creates battles within people or with others, it causes inner feelings of conflict and ill will. In contrast, true spirituality creates inner calmness, compassion, tolerance, and kindness.

> *"My religion is kindness. I have found that the greatest degree of inner tranquility comes from the development of love and compassion. The more we care for the happiness of others, the greater our own sense of well being. It is the principal source of success in life."*
> —Dalai Lama

In organized religion, conformity is often required. You might want to consider whether it feels better to seek your own path, rather than a path dictated by someone else.

"Why become a Buddhist, when you can become a Buddha?"
—Lama Surya Das

"Religion is a set of rules that defines someone else's spiritual experience. Spirituality is experiencing your own."
—Mastin Kipp

"Religion is cultural mythology. Spirituality is self awareness The two have nothing in common."
—Deepak Chopra

What do all religions have in common? They are made up of thought. All religions are both false and true, depending on whether they are used in the service of the ego or in the service of the truth. If you believe that only your religion is the truth, you are using it in the service of the ego. Used in truth, religious teachings become signposts left behind by enlightened individuals to aid you in your quest of spiritual awakening.

"The finger pointing at the moon is not the moon"
—Buddhist teaching

There are many positive outcomes from organized religion. Some of the work that church groups perform helps humanity. Also, the joining together of people for a common cause can produce good energy and health. To collectively believe can also provide comfort, as can the camaraderie of a strong support group.

Religion should be a remedy to help reduce conflict and suffering in the world...not be the source of rivalry. The purpose of religion should be to benefit people, to nourish the human spirit. So many things divide humanity; religion should not be among them. True spirituality is a mental attitude that you can practice any time. For example, when you are about to get angry, remind yourself that animosity is not a spiritual practice... and that every event is an opportunity to learn.

"To make this whole world a big family, an ocean of love is the only religion I can think of."
—Osho

It would be extraordinary to live in a spiritual society where every individual realized we are all connected to the same source. As long as we keep devaluing or killing other people we decide we "don't like" or "are wrong" we are drifting further and further from our own spirituality. I resist using the word "God," because the meaning has become so distorted. It was man who created God in his own image. The infinite, the eternal, the un-nameable was reduced to an idol that you had to believe in or worship as "my God" or "your God." Even belief in God is a poor substitute for the reality of God manifesting in every moment of your life.

Significantly, if we allow ourselves to believe that there is no "my God" and "your God," mankind could stop fighting with each other simply because they have different belief systems, and each individual would be free to embark on his or her own spiritual path. There are billions of different points of view, but it is all the same light, the same energy, the same force behind each and every one of us. *When we allow the freedom of choice to everyone, and we accept the responsibility for our flexibility to choose our own thoughts and beliefs...we as a society will have achieved spirituality and emotional fitness.*

I believe this is what Jesus called "Heaven on Earth," Buddha called "Nirvana," and Moses called "The Promised Land." Can you imagine what kind of world this would be if all people opened their hearts and found the love inside? Everyone can do it in his or her own way. It's not about following any imposed idea. It is about finding yourself. You are here because of the power of God, the power of Life, the power of Creation. Just be aware, make a choice, and work through your fears. You'll find that the only thing left is Love and Compassion.

> *"Heaven is right here in the midst of you."*
> —Jesus

> *"I honor the place within you where the entire Universe resides;*
> *I honor the place within you of love, of light, of truth, of peace; I*
> *honor the place within you, where, when you are in that place in*
> *you, and I am in that place in me, there is only one of us."*
> —Namaste'...As defined by Mahatma Gandhi

5.5 PARENTING

We have discussed groups that seek to control you. What about children, who we, as adults, control to some extent. Do we take to heart this huge responsibility?

Biology of Belief, by Bruce Lipton, explains how important conscious parenting is from conception to 6 years old (Chapter 7, *Conscious Parenting: Parents as Genetic Engineers*). Lipton uses Associazione Nazionale Educazione Prenatale, an Italian conscious parenting organization, to illustrate the importance of conscious parenting with a video of a fetus in the womb, seen with sonogram, jumping when its parents begin arguing. When the argument is punctuated by the shattering of glass, the fetus arches its back and jumps up as if it were on a trampoline.

During a child's first seven or eight years, its mind absorbs all information without question. It is during this time that the beliefs and values that will be with the child throughout his or her life are formed. These include beliefs about who they are and what the world represents to them. Also encompassed are beliefs about success and failure, right and wrong, good and bad, love, money, charity, etc.

Why do you think young children ask so many questions? To drive adults crazy? It is because they are constantly making evaluations about what things mean and the way to react. They are creating the connections in their brains that will guide their futures. These same connections were made by you or were made for you by others when you were young.

It is not until a child is around eight years old that the critical faculty begins to form. The critical faculty is the part of the brain that chooses to distinguish between reality and fantasy. That is when the child begins to question information and starts to draw his or her own conclusions. Fundamentally, the patterns that were established in the previous 8 years will filter how the child sees the world.

When the child has reached the early teens, direct access to the unconscious mind has been sealed by the critical faculty, and the choices that the young adult will make are dictated by the unconscious mind. (More on this in the previous chapter: Your Unconscious Mind). During the early years, the unconscious mind creates a particularly deep connection with beliefs caused by traumatic experiences, because those are the beliefs that we assume helped us survive or deal with these events.

Beliefs can be developed based on times in your childhood when you felt judged, criticized, or not accepted. If an excited and enthusiastic child is instructed to be quiet, the fragment that is enthusiastic may shut down. This could result in the child having difficulty expressing or even feeling enthusiasm as they mature. What if the child learns that they have to "be good" to avoid their parents' disappointment and to feel loved? As an adult, they continue this pattern by becoming a people pleaser, often sacrificing their own values or needs....or they may suffer from perfectionism, where they are never satisfied by their own performance unless it is perfect.

Beliefs can also be based on positive experiences, such as a child saying something funny that makes people laugh. Children can be encouraged to feel they can do anything because they received praise for accomplishments. Beliefs can be as simple as knowing they were loved, even if they did not fulfill expectations.

We have countless opportunities to instill belief systems in children that will aid them in their growth. There may also be occasions where, due to our own beliefs, we implant belief systems in children that stunt their growth. For example, children are born with the ability to swim, but acquire a fear of water from their parents. As a result of this, the biggest hurdle in teaching children to swim is overcoming the fear that was introduced previously.

In *Mens Health Magazine*, March 2012, actor Jesse Eisenberg tells the story of how his mother instilled his fear of water, by telling him she had nightmares of him drowning. When he went to camp and took swimming lessons, he followed every instruction but failed at swimming. He never attributed his inability to swim to his mother's nightmares; he just assumed his body did not have the swimming instinct. Going through life without swimming was not a problem, and when he joined the YMCA with his girlfriend, he avoided the pool. Then, while getting into character for a role he was to play, he decided that his reckless character, "Billy" knew how to swim. When he got into the pool, he awkwardly waded towards the ladder like he used to do in camp, but then "Billy" dominated his actions. Thinking like Billy, or more importantly, not thinking like himself, allowed him to overcome a bad habit he did not even realize he had. He competed in the 100 meter butterfly in the 2012 Summer Olympics.

"I assumed that more than 4 million years of
evolution must have stopped at me."
—Jesse Eisenberg

That is just one example. What belief systems have stunted you? What belief systems are you instilling in your children that will stunt them? What learned perceptions are you programming to your children that have thwarted your emotional fitness, and will in turn thwart theirs? What positive beliefs are you introducing to your children that will aid them in their quest for emotional fitness?

In school, children are taught to memorize the dates of famous battles in our wars...but their education does not always encompass how to function as happy productive adults. Children learn that war is a natural part of life... that humans are warlike by nature. Let's teach children that we need to discover other ways to address our issues...and that cooperation yields better results and war may not be necessary.

"Children are sent off to school to make credits and to learn
how to memorize, not to learn what they want in life."
—Napoleon Hill

As a result of the need for funding, schools have become more concerned with test scores than with actually preparing children to function in the real world. As a result, it is especially important for anyone who is, or is planning to be a parent, to realize that it is his/her responsibility to be a positive influence on his/her children.

So, what do we do? Realize it is impossible to be a perfect parent, but do your best while protecting your children from the scars of your own childhood. Your children watch how you treat others, your charitable values, and your general outlook on life. They will have interpretations of everything you say and do. Be sure that you are exemplifying the qualities and values that you aspire your children to copy, because your children will mimic your behavior and adopt how you relate to other people and the world. If you are not already as confident in these areas as you would like, you can form some good habits for yourself in the process. **If you want your children to grow up with emotional fitness... start with yourself.**

"*You are the bows from which your children as living arrows are sent forth. The Archer sees the mark upon the path of the infinite, and He bends with you, with His might that His arrows may go swift and far. Let your bending in the archers hand be for gladness; For even as he loves the arrow that flies, so He loves the bow that is stable.*"
—Kahlil Gibran

6. UNDERSTANDING GOALS

*C*hances are, at some point in your life, you have set goals. But, before you knew it, your motivation was gone and you were fighting to stay on track. This chapter shows you several different ways to decide on and achieve your goals.

The biggest problem with setting goals is the "let's get there fast" mentality. The goal setting causes you to focus on the future moment when you will attain your goal, forcing you to lose touch with the present.

In striving for a goal or outcome, avoid getting into a rigid mindset at the expense of your creativity. When the goal becomes more important than the process of working towards it, your life becomes a means to an end, an obstacle, or a battle.

Your relationship with the present moment is your relationship with life. The table below shows six different levels at which you interact with life:

Enthusiasm
Enjoyment
Acceptance
Means to an end
Obstacle
Battle

When you live below the line, treating the present moment as a means to an end or an obstacle, you throwaway "now" for the sake of "maybe". When the future moment arrives that you sacrificed the present moment for, you end up treating that moment the same way, and strive for another future moment where you believe your happiness lies. If you sink even further and treat the present moment as a battle, life will respond to you in kind. It will be as if life is saying to you... *if war is what you want, war is what you will get.*

When you live above the line, you accept the present moment in whatever form it takes, and then take action from that place. Life is very simple. It happens in front of you, and you get to choose how you wish to interact. When you interact by accepting whatever form life takes, joy is inevitable. Enthusiasm sets in while working towards a worthwhile goal. However, the moment that the goal becomes more important than the process of working towards it, your life has been reduced to a means to an end, an obstacle, or a battle.

> *"Happiness is the progressive realization of a worthy goal."*
> —Deepak Chopra

The key is to be focused on but not attached to the outcome. Not being attached to an outcome does not take away from your goals; it adds to them because it allows you to manifest what you want in an enjoyable and stress-free way. Being attached to an outcome, in contrast, may cause stress and a loss of creativity. When we take the pressure off ourselves to produce results at any cost and instead follow our inner wisdom and our trust in the process of life, events often unfold better than we could have ever imagined.

> *"In order to acquire anything in the physical Universe, you must first relinquish your attachment to it. You don't give up the intention and you don't give up the desire. You give up your attachment to the result".*
> —Deepak Chopra

Another problem is that people set goals in a forced state. For example, overwhelmed by money problems, you set an objective to get rich. Great idea…except while your conscious mind is focused on the goal of getting rich, your unconscious mind is consumed by the underlying problems your thoughts are generating…lack of money. Or, if you are upset with your weight and set a goal to diet, your unconscious is upset and giving energy to being overweight while your conscious tries to accomplish the goal of reducing. I think you know how this turns out.

Another example is setting a goal to resist bad food and forcing yourself to eat healthy. You can use willpower to resist the pleasure of the food and tolerate the pain of depriving yourself, but your actions will be short-lived because they go against the way you are programmed. We are all programmed to seek pleasure and avoid pain. So instead, choose to see the pain of over indulgence and feel how rewarding it is to have control over yourself. Visualize a lot of positive outcomes from the chosen behavior. The key here is to assign a feeling of pleasure to the behaviors you desire, and a feeling of pain to those that are undesired.

"I believe that pleasures are to be avoided if greater pains are the consequence, and pains be coveted if they will terminate in greater pleasures."
—Michel De Montaigne

Think about a goal you have. Next...move it from your mind to your heart. How do you feel about it? How do you feel when you think about it already being achieved? When you hit obstacles, will you let them be excuses, challenges, or opportunities? Now...resolve to enjoy the process of moving towards that which you want, and become as clear as possible as to what is in your control and what is not. People cause themselves pain trying to control things over which they have no control. Resolve that you'll be okay no matter the outcome, and that your identity and ultimate happiness are not tied to the result. If you are pursuing actions that make you happy and fulfilled instead of a "goal", you are free from "failure" because you aren't tied to strict deadlines and specific outcomes. You can be successful right now!

Of course there will always be disappointments, frustrations, setbacks, and even failures... that is just part of life. But in those challenging times you can still have an inner sense of calm and joy... know that you can weather any storm...and come out on the other side not only okay...but wiser, stronger, and better off from the experience.

"What lies behind us and what lies before us are small matters compared to what lies within us."
—Ralph Wald Emerson

Understand the difference between "moving toward" and "moving away from" goals. A "moving toward"goal involves moving toward something desirable and a "moving away from"goal is when you are moving away from something undesirable. Moving away from goals are less effective, because the further away you get from what you don't want, the lower your motivation becomes. For example, if your goal is to lose weight, the further you get away from your current weight will result in you being less motivated. Conversely, if your goal is to move towards a healthy weight, getting closer increases your motivation because your goal is getting closer. Similarly, if you no longer want money struggles, the further you distance from your struggles; the less you will be motivated. But if your goal is to acquire wealth, the closer you get to wealth elevates your encouragement and desire.

Sometimes when desired results are not being achieved, people focus on negative thoughts and problems, and look for ways to blame themselves, other people, or situations. Focusing on the negative makes you feel bad because it orients you towards failure. If instead you focus on what you desire, why you want it, how you will know when you have it, how achieving this positive outcome will improve your life, and what resources you can use to accomplish it, you are more likely to achieve the ultimate outcome.

Focus on what you do want, and you will be on the path of infinite possibilities, because your core energy will be in harmony with your outer goal.

Often people have an idea of what they want, but their vision is so vague that they have difficulty knowing what to do to attain their goal and when they have actually succeeded. Perhaps the most important question to ask yourself is "What type of person will I need to become to achieve the goal I have chosen?"

"First say to yourself what you would be; and then
do what you have to do."
—Epictetus

For instance, suppose your desired outcome is to be "better at dealing with my child." The vision for accomplishing this goal is that your voice is calm and even, you are honestly communicating your concerns, and you take into account your child's feelings and insecurities. In specifying this outcome you may realize that you know little or nothing about your child's insecurities and you then realize you need to devote some time and energy to understanding that particular aspect of your overall outcome.

When you focus on the outcome you desire, and picture the result so you will know when you have achieved it, your chances of capturing what you want are greatly enhanced, as is your joy of the journey towards it.

"People with goals succeed because they know where they're going."
—Earl Nightingale

Think of something you want and ask yourself "Why do I want that?" Basically, we want certain things because we see them as a way to obtain desired feelings or emotional states. With that in mind...

Five step process to achieving any goal.

1. Think of a goal.
2. How will achieving that goal make you feel?
3. Picture yourself already feeling that way.
4. Understand that the real goal is step 3.
5. Realize that this feeling is accessible to you now.

"If you don't know where you are going,
you might wind up someplace else."
—Yogi Berra

7. MONEY

*L*ike it or not, we live in a world that revolves around money. Be sure you understand that money is a representation of energy. The energy that you expel to create goods or services is traded for energy that someone else exudes to create something you want. In the days before there was money, people would literally trade goods or services. Then, as our civilization grew, money made it simpler to barter our energy.

It is essential to understand your motivations towards money. The first question to ask yourself is…What does money mean to me? What does money provide for me? Allow your thoughts and do not judge them. Are your thoughts based on fear or love?

> *"Money is like sex…I only worry about it when I don't have any."*
> —Rick Lawson

To an extent, money does make you happier, because with no money, you have nothing to trade for the things that you want. If you do not have the basics of food, shelter and health care, money becomes paramount to your happiness and well being.

The problem arrives when no matter how much money you have, you forget gratitude and simply want more. When people of various income levels were asked how much money they need to be happy, people making $20,000 per year thought $30,000 would be sufficient… and people making $100,000 per year thought $200,000 per year was necessary, and I'm guessing that people making $500,000 per year would feel that life would exponentially change if they only had a million.

> *"Money never made a man happy yet, nor will it…*
> *instead of filling a vacuum, it makes one.*
> *If it satisfies one want, it doubles and triples that want in another way."*
> —Benjamin Franklin

*"People spend money they don't have, on things they
don't need, to impress people they don't like."*
—George Fokas

When people around the world are asked about their satisfaction with life, affluent countries score higher, possibly because their lives are easier. But when the same people are asked if they are happy in the moment, one of the poorest countries, Nigeria, scored highest.... followed by Mexico, Venezuela, El Salvador, Puerto Rico, Vietnam, and Cambodia. This evidences that more money does not necessarily create happier people. We could also hypothesize that people in poor countries have better relationships, because their relationships are with people instead of material things. People in modern affluent countries connect more through social media and text messaging. Possibly these digital connections and their resulting relationships are wreaking havoc on our interpersonal skills and enjoyment of our peers.

*"Electric communication will never be a substitute for the face of someone
who with their soul encourages another person to be brave and true."*
—Charles Dickens

When people envision that more money creates happiness, they have hope. Then, when these same people achieve wealth and are still not happy, that hope is lost. If you have learned anything from this book, it is that happiness is created on the inside. Money only affects what is on the outside. Is the aim in life to see how much stuff you can acquire?

"It's one thing to choose Abundance...it's another thing to need it."
—Bruce D Schneider

*"And what is fear of need but need itself? Is not dread of thirst
when your well is full, the thirst that is unquenchable?"*
—Kahlil Gibran

Even if you win the lottery, you probably will not be much happier then you are now unless you change your inner perceptions. According to research done by Harvard psychologist Dan Gilbert, a person's state of mind is not significantly affected by life changing events, such as winning the lottery or becoming a paraplegic. *"The fact is that a year after losing the use of their legs and a year after winning the lottery, lottery winners and paraplegics are equally happy with their lives as they were before."* (on TED.com)

When an individual defines themselves by who they are rather than what they possess, life becomes much easier and happier...because they see their true worth. Your true value is never tied to your bank account or what you have acquired, it is always connected to who you are and the energy you radiate as a human being. How do you measure success? Here's how I measure it...True wealth is a state of mind, a state of emotional fitness.

> *"There is a saying in Tibetan that "at the door of the miserable rich man sleeps the contented beggar." The point of this saying is not that poverty is a virtue, but that happiness does not come from wealth, but from setting limits to one's desires, and living within those limits with satisfaction."*
> —Dalai Lama

The biggest complication comes when you unconsciously trade something of greater value for money. Ask yourself "is the money more important than what I am losing for it? What values am I honoring with this decision? What values am I violating"?

> *"The essence of wealth is life energy"*
> —Deepak Chopra

The Dalai Lama, when asked what surprised him most about humanity, answered:

> *"Man. Because he sacrifices his health in order to make money. Then he sacrifices money in order to recuperate his health. And then he is so anxious about the future that he does not enjoy the present; the result being that he does not live in the present or the future; he lives as if he is never going to die, and then he dies having never really lived."*

A challenge people might face regarding money is mixed emotions or mixed associations. For example, often we associate an increase in wealth with aspects of freedom, yet also associate a loss of choice or even a change of character...therefore the signals to the unconscious are mixed. There is little doubt that most people desire more money and have lots of good reasons on a conscious level, but if deep down they associate having too much money with problems, these beliefs could prevent achieving increased wealth. In fact, if someone who lacks money incorporates negative judgments about affluent people, they send these harmful messages to their unconscious and thereby sabotage their conscious desire for financial freedom. Bottom line: *Be careful how you evaluate the world around you, as the unconscious mind looks to the conscious for direction.* Also, when you make negative judgments about those to whom you may be envious, you are sending instructions to your unconscious to follow a different path.

> *"While others may sidetrack your ambitions a few times, remember that discouragement most frequently comes from within."*
> —Napoleon Hill

People who don't have enough money may also be asking themselves the wrong questions. They might ask "What could I buy right now" instead of "What long term planning should I commence to create the abundance that I deserve?" Fear based questions are disempowering, but with fear in mind, an empowering question might be "What is the worst that could happen with this project, and could I handle that?" As you learned in earlier chapters...ask the right questions, get the right answers.

What about your beliefs and self talk? If you truly believe that you *want* more money...you will probably continue to *want* more money, because the *want* is where you are putting your energy. Instead, decide the person you would be if you had the wealth you desire, and approach life from that place. Remember, it is never a matter of what you are doing...it is always a matter of what you are being.

People who chase money for security will usually not obtain the peace they are looking for, because security can never come from money alone. Attachment to money may in fact create insecurity, a fear that the wealth will not continue. Importantly, security does not come from certainty, but rather from a willingness to accept the uncertainty that life will always present. By accepting uncertainty, you are on the path to freedom, and you will interpret all problems as the seeds of an opportunity.

"Give the world the best you have and the best will come back to you."
—Madeline Bridges

The good news is that more money can make you happier. If you are already satisfied on the inside, with a good self image and a compassion for others, increased income will allow you to do and be so much more. It can provide you a freedom you have never known. If you choose to embark on a path to achieve lots of money, remember this along the way...

"You can have prosperity no matter what your present circumstances may be."
—Emmet Fox

If you have a desire for more money, first discover your true self and how you can express your unique talents to fulfill the needs of others. Focus on what you have to offer so you can enjoy yourself in the process. Think about what you might want to accomplish if you already had all the money you want.

"What I wanted was to be able to be allowed to do the
thing in the world that I did best – which I believed then
and believe now is the greatest privilege there is."
—Debbie Fields (Mrs. Fields Cookies)

Now ask yourself how engaged you are in your quest. If you are not at a 10 (on a scale of 1-10), ask yourself what beliefs you need to acquire to get that level of desire. If you cannot get to a 10, realize that there are more important things to you than making lots of money, and be at peace with that choice.

If you are at a 10, do you believe, with all your heart, that you can achieve wealth? If not, your beliefs will hold you back. What will you need to do to fully assimilate that you can obtain and sustain wealth? You will need to figure that out and get to that place of understanding.

With your desire at a 10 and your belief at a 10...how will you feel when you have met your wealth goal? From that feeling, accept that you have already achieved what you intended. When you start from the right level of consciousness, the right thoughts arise. We are not talking about the law of attraction; we are talking about the law of being. Everything begins from your level of consciousness.

The next and final step is to take action. When you mix the right level of desire, belief, and acceptance with an empowered level of action you are on the course to achievement, because you now have no inner blocks...and any outer blocks will be overcome by this very powerful version of you.

> *"The vision must be followed by the venture.*
> *It is not enough to stare up the steps - we must step up the stairs."*
> —Vance Havner

Remember: You decide what success means. You decide what winning is. You decide what the rules are.

> *"If you want to feel rich,*
> *just count all of the things you have that money can't buy."*
> —Anonymous

> *"If you are poor, live wisely. If you have riches, live wisely.*
> *It is not your station in life but your heart that brings blessings."*
> —Buddha

8. WORK AND BUSINESS

*L*ike other flows, if the energy flow within yourself is not free to flow out, then the flow in is hindered. In order to achieve the free passage of energy through the body and mind that creates the feelings we call bliss, love, inner peace, and contentment, it is of paramount importance to keep the flow going.

In this light, "work" (the outflow of energy) takes on a whole new meaning. We learn that it is good to work for works sake, not just for the fruits of our labor. This is because, simply by working, we are enhancing our energy flow, and therefore achieving optimal states of being.

> *"Work is love made visible. And if you cannot work with love but only with distaste, it is better that you should leave your work and sit at the gate of the temple and take alms of those who work with joy."*
> —Kahlil Gibran

Success is achieved by mastering its components. In other words, get rid of your baggage, have the right attitude, acquire the right skills, understand selling, create efficient and effective systems, practice leadership, embrace customer service, and develop rapport. Most importantly, remember this: You cannot become successful, you can only be successful. Do not let anyone ever tell you that success is anything other than a successful present moment.

> *"Success in life could be defined as the continued expansion of happiness and the progressive realization of worthy goals."*
> —Deepak Chopra

Get Rid of Baggage: If you set a goal without releasing your baggage (the conditioned beliefs and belief systems which no longer benefit you) your reality will be filtered through your shortcomings. Get rid of your impediments and learn about yourself and how you function by reading books like the one you are holding in your hands right now.

The Right Attitude: Some good mindsets include curiosity, gratitude, persistence, generosity, integrity, self-respect, ambition, passion, courage, resilience, optimism, and concern for the welfare of others. The right perspective also includes a willingness to learn and to hold yourself accountable for your actions.

The Right Skills: Acquire any special skills needed for your chosen endeavor. If you are a carpenter you need different expertise than a doctor. In addition to specialized accomplishments, everyone requires certain universal skills to be successful. You need people skills, self-management skills, organization skills, and the skills of marketing your business successfully or the skills to find, motivate, and work with someone who has these skills. No business can succeed without customers, so all of your business skills need to serve the purpose of attracting and satisfying customers.

Understand Selling: The key to selling is to ask the right questions so you can articulate your customers' problem or needs better than they can. Create instant rapport by asking questions, which shows you care. Good doctors ask questions and then repeat back what they learn to make sure they understand clearly.

This can be called pulling instead of pushing. (Of course, that's not all there is to it – there are some critical steps afterwards you need to take including asking for the sale, but EVERYTHING you will do means little if you get this step wrong.)

Bottom line: Instead of trying to sell something, realize that you are conducting a personal interview with a human being who is attempting to find out if you offer something that he/she perceives as a need or a want.

Create Efficient and Effective Systems: An efficient and flexible system will not attempt to change the nature of the people so that the system will work better, but instead will change itself so that it can more efficiently harness the energy flow that is actually taking place. In other words, create the systems around the people, don't try to create the people around the systems.

Practice leadership: The role of a leader is not to come up with the best ideas or to be the smartest person in the room, but instead to create an environment where great ideas can happen and others will become brilliant. It is the people "in the trenches" who are most qualified to find the best method of performance. When people are told to do their job, that is all they will do. But when they are united behind a common cause, vision, or goal, they will do much more than their job. This is because they will know the *why* instead of just the *what*. Many companies have star employees, but great leadership will create a culture that produces great people as a rule and not an exception.

> *"When the great leaders work is done, the people say* 'we did it ourselves'"
> —*Sun Tzu*

Embrace Customer Service: The two most important words when serving others are "compassion" and "empathy." When you genuinely serve with compassion and empathy, your customer service is unsurpassable.

Your customers are not rational when their emotions overpower their reasoning abilities. Watching a customer react unreasonably to something we perceive as minor can be very confusing and frustrating. However, when a customer has expectations (reasonable or not) and we fail to deliver, emotions are a likely result.

Once we understand there is a good probability of a person reacting emotionally instead of rationally, we need to choose to not take it personally, thereby remaining in our thinking mind instead of reacting emotionally ourselves. This allows us to serve with compassion and empathy, which provides everyone, including ourselves, with a superior experience.

Develop Rapport with Everyone: Rapport is a harmonious relationship between two or more people. This happens when people are in sync or on the same wavelength, resulting in them feeling similar and/or relating well to each other. It is much easier to reach an understanding to resolve differences when rapport is established. Events will run smoothly when people are on the same wavelength.

Make a conscious decision that you want to be in sync with whomever you are interacting. This decision tells your whole body how to behave.

> *"Act as if you were confident, optimistic and outgoing.*
> *You'll manage adversity, rise to the occasion, create instant connections,*
> *make friends and influence people, and become a happier person."*
> —Sonja Lyupomirsky

Make eye contact and notice and use the other person's name. Match the tone and pace of their talking, and notice and share their energy level.

Commonality will breed rapport...we always are more comfortable with people that are like us.

I observed a good example of rapport while managing my health club. A member came in and was very upset. I could see the front desk and I heard the receptionist say "Wow...that's terrible...wait just a second." Then she walked back and told me that this member had been charged when he had put his membership on hold. I walked out to the front desk and said "Hi, My name is Gary...how can I help?"

The man was completely calm as he told me what happened and how much the girl at the front desk had helped him. After I fixed the problem for him, I got to thinking...what had she done to help him?

What she had done, without even realizing it, was to share in his outrage. She showed this by matching his demeanor when he complained. And he was comforted...which resulted in him liking her and ceasing to be angry. All because she unknowingly created rapport by matching his behavior.

Something that we all have in common is that we want to be understood. We want to love and be loved. And we all want to be "okay". You can ask yourself, "What must be going on in this person's world for their statements and actions to make sense and be true for them?" This question will help you find the compassion, understanding and resulting rapport which will then "smooth out" the interaction. Sometimes it may be helpful to look within and ask yourself the same question.

We are always sending out energy about things as to which we are most aware – whether it is our likenesses or differences. Are you focused on how different the other person is from you or can you concentrate on how you are basically alike? What you focus on will determine the energy you send out into the world around you.

And when you have the chance, give a little to everyone. Offer kind words and contribute appreciation, love, and compliments. Award courtesy wherever you go. You can supply not just a smile, but also a warm greeting to all of the people with whom you come in contact. Bestow warm embraces to those you love. Allow appreciation and encouragement to everyone, including yourself.

> "Communication is merely an exchange of information,
> but connection is an exchange of our humanity."
> —Sean Stephenson

9. YOUR INNER FAMILY

Who is your Inner Family? Are they a group of cheerleaders, mentors, coaches, and co-creators, or do the nay-sayers, ne'er do-wells, and critical parents drown out the positive messages? There are patterns within us, sometimes called archetypes. They are neither good or bad, as there is a time and a place for each one. The six main personalities within you are your inner child, villain, victim, hero, prostitute, and saboteur; and they are discussed in detail below. Knowing and understanding these six components of your identity will help you to become aware when they emerge, allowing you to experience the opportunities each one can bring into your life.

Your Inner Child - When you say "I always" that reveals the inner child within you recreating your reality as a child. When you say "I don't deserve that" recognize it is the opinion of your inner child. If you are not letting go of resentment, it is your inner child saying "If I don't forgive yesterday, I won't have any pain tomorrow".

Sometimes when a child doesn't obtain what it wants...it will pout and throw tantrums. When an adult flies into a rage or gets so angry as to lose control...or pouts when not getting his/her way...it is the re-emergence of that child.

If your inner child seeks parental energy, you will look to a partner to make the world safe. Recognize the patterns within you that motivate your choices.

A dynamic that will never serve you is the need for someone else's approval. When you seek approval, it is your inner child. People can be afraid to give you approval because by doling out approval they may perceive they are giving you power. Empower yourself.

Whenever you "beat yourself up" it's probably your inner child. It was as a child that you received criticism and took it to heart. Speak to yourself with the kindness and compassion that you would use to address a child. You are the adult in your life now, and if you are not comforting the child within you, you are not advancing towards your emotional fitness.

Your Inner Victim - Your inner victim causes you to live in fear, and challenging the inner victim helps you develop self esteem. Your inner victim alerts you to possibilities of being victimized. "Never again" is a victim phrase. When you are given an idea, your inner victim will want to imagine how this could victimize you so it will examine your history to find a wound from your past.

A relationship is an exchange of power...so if an ex-mate still has power over you, they are making your choices for you. You feel victimized because you have given your power to someone else. Also, the victim in you fears being alone. Because of this you may be in a relationship not only for love's sake...but also because your partner has some energy that you need.

Use your inner victim for information and awareness, but then designate the part of you to make choices going forward. Emotionally fit people do not choose to be victims, they gather information from their inner victim, and then select to move forward as a victor instead.

Your Inner Villain - An inner villain may result from a strict upbringing. It can stem from a rebellious nature. This archetype manifests in harmless pranks and rebellious behavior, possibly due to an inability to conform to other people's rules (not necessarily a bad thing). An inner villain can also arise from anger deep inside. As discussed in the Anger chapter, people that are angry are in pain, and they enjoy sharing that pain. Like the victim, the villain is living in fear. In fact, there are many similarities between the victim and the villain.

Your Inner Hero - Perhaps you were victimized in the past, so now the hero persona fits you better. That's fine, unless the hero takes over and you are not aware of the reality of a situation and your motivations. Playing the hero can be a mask to cover up insecurities. It can come from a need to prove your worth. When you have a compulsion to be the hero, make sure you know from where the motivation arises.

Your Inner Prostitute - An example of your inner prostitute is believing that being with a particular person is necessary for your well being, so you do things or put up with things you normally would not, to keep that person around. Another example is when you hate your job but resist leaving, or when you believe your well being comes from your job and income, so you overinvest your time and betray your values to keep or enhance that job. We use survival as an excuse for violating our values. It is important to remember that your inner prostitute does not cost you your inner power unless you are lying to yourself. As long as you are making conscious choices out of awareness of your values, do not judge, as there is an inner prostitute in all of us.

Your Inner Saboteur will find the weakest link in any situation and tell you why it will fail. How many ways do you tell yourself things cannot be done? You will most likely meet your saboteur when you are trying to create change in your life. The way to get past your saboteur is to ask yourself…what is the worst possible truth I could find out about myself?

Your different personalities work together; an example is when the victim fears being alone and the child fears abandonment. The child will be afraid while the victim feels disadvantaged. Another example is when the victim and the saboteur get together…you become paralyzed with fear.

Role playing based on your Inner Family is an unconscious dance occurring every day between you and the people with whom you interact. How do we overcome these tendencies? Start from a powerful place, which is a detached level of emotional involvement. Passively observe and trust that it is all part of the process of life. Anxiety is a result of not trusting the path that your life is taking.

While managing my health club (and before I found emotional fitness), I would don my cape and fly into the hero role if I observed someone being rude to a receptionist. I flew into the role of hero to the person I perceived as the victim. I became a bigger villain than the villain himself, thereby turning the villain into a victim. As the conflict ended and each of our roles were reinforced, we continued on with our different interactions with others throughout the day. If you are thinking about the villain being turned into a victim when I said that our roles were reinforced…please remember what you learned in the chapter *What are you thinking about?*, that people become the villain out of a fear of being the victim. When I attacked the villain, his fear was then realized as the villain was victimized, further reinforcing those fears…and making the villain into an even more powerful villain next time, saying "I won't let that happen again."

What can we learn from this example? If I hadn't needed to be the hero and had passively observed and let the scene play out, both parties might have learned a lesson about themselves or about how to better deal with such a situation. If I observed that it still wasn't resolving…I could have stepped in only as a conscious observer, not an unconscious hero, and helped both parties to understand the events that were developing. As you have hopefully learned …conflicts do not arise from what is happening, only due to people's perceptions of what is transpiring…and by changing the perception, we change the emotions and thus the outcome.

"It is possible for the unconscious or an archetype to take complete possession of a man and to determine his fate down to the smallest detail"
—Carl Jung

Become conscious of the roles you play based on the personalities of your Inner Family, as they will influence the choices you make. Also think about these roles in relation to how you interact with others. If you are the hero to a victim, realize that if you were less of a hero they might be less of a victim. If you are a repeated victim to a villain, understand that you have been unconsciously comfortable in that role. Now that you are conscious...what will your choice be? Being aware of these personalities, as well as any other personalities within you, helps you gain strength from them instead of weakness.

What will you choose when you silence them...or learn from them? What decisions will you make when you are empowered, rather than letting fear make your choices?

When your unconscious co-creates your reality...your conscious mind is left to pick up the pieces. Start from a place of consciousness. Emotional fitness is when you are aware of all that goes into your selections, so you can make your choices from a place of empowerment.

"We all have the archetype inside us of the enlightened being"
—Dan Millman

10. ADDICTIONS

In this chapter we will not be addressing medical addictions. Instead, we discuss addictions as behaviors that control you, in which you participate, either consciously or unconsciously. These addictions are usually symptoms of deeper problems. When symptoms are treated without isolating the root problem, the symptom will usually return. The purpose of this chapter is to make you aware of any addictions that exist within you. Some addictions are: attitudes, self pity (martyr), needing to be right, exercise, needing to control others, judging, being critical, self criticism, needing approval, being beyond reason, rebellion, and of course, alcohol, drugs, and food.

> *"Addictions stem from looking for God in all the wrong places."*
> —Mastin Kipp

First, connect with your strength and confidence, instead of reaching for short term symptom relief, and thereby attack the root of the problem. An example of symptom relief is when an ostrich sticks its head in the sand, thinking it is avoiding what it fears. You need to be willing to unite with your inner strength and confidence instead of just performing based on habits and patterns.

> *"Every addiction arises from an unconscious refusal to face and move through your own pain…you are using something or somebody to cover up your pain."*
> —Eckhart Tolle

It is not always an either/or proposition, like either you give in to the craving or resist. You have other choices…such as to walk away, postpone, find a distraction, pause and reflect, or substitute another pleasure.

It's not so much about defeating the craving, but about gradually creating a new program in your brain. Struggle only makes the conditioning worse because you are focusing on and repeating the same conflict over and over. Remember your neuro pathways and the river or gym cable metaphors from chapter 2.8 (Your Self Image).

Sometimes there are two voices in your head. One says, go ahead and give in to the craving, while the other one promotes resistance. The arguing of these two voices can lead to an obsession.

If you are feeling bad for giving in to a craving, connect with your feelings. Realize that giving in to your dependence never works. Find out what you really want. Is it love, comfort, approval, or security?

Cravings and addictions are a substitute for these feelings, and each time you substitute the sensation for the addictive behavior, the addiction loses its grip.

"The tough thing about learning self discipline
is that we need self discipline in order to learn it."
—Glenn Van Ekeren

Living in Harmony

An addiction is making the same decision over and over again. You cannot break an addiction with just your head or just your heart, because your heart will seek an emotional reason to continue and your mind will try to find a logical consideration. Your heart will provide excuses while your mind provides denial. In between all of this activity is you...not knowing how to respond.

When your head and your heart make different decisions, you are creating two realities at the same time. Uniting your heart and mind creates harmony and power. The end result is a being without internal conflict. Without a unified will, the mind finds an addiction to help it feel stable, or distracted from the conflict within.

"The longest journey that you will make in your life
is from your heart to your head."
—Gary Zucov, The Heart Of the Soul

Every thought and every word is a choice. How many decisions do you make each day that cancel each other out? When you rebel, you don't know who you are...just who you don't want to be. As long as you are an addict you can blame someone else. When you are in harmony, you cease blaming. When you are in harmony, conscious denial is no longer a desired option.

If you have a lot to forgive (of yourself or others), then you have a lot of your energy in your history...so you are more likely to be an addict.

Addictions that alter your consciousness may stem from an inability to forgive. Alcohol, drugs, and food can be addictions caused by wounds.

Addictions such as work and exercise are addictions of the ego. Ego addictions are essentially an obsession with a high social order. Other examples include addictions to image and lifestyle.

> *"The publicly virtuous have found a new ego addiction…*
> *one that makes them look better than they are."*
> —*Deepak Chopra*

Can a person, habit, or substance exert more power over your choices than you do? If your answer is yes… or that it's a struggle… you have an addiction. If you have surrendered to an addiction, you have lost your choice.

If you want to quit smoking, you have to fall in love with fresh air. If you want to quit drugs, you have to embrace the feeling of total consciousness and awareness. If you want to quit overeating, adore the benefits of being at a healthy weight.

We all suffer from addictions…that's just part of being human, but we can substitute a positive addiction for a negative one, or choose consciously which addictions serve our life purpose. Being in harmony and making your own powerful evaluations, from both your heart and your head… that's emotional fitness.

———

Here's an interesting story about an interaction between a retired policeman and the **legendary hypnotist Milton Erickson**:

"I have emphysema, high blood pressure, and, as you can see, I am grossly overweight. I drink too much. I eat too much. I want a job but my emphysema and blood pressure prevent that. I would like to cut down on my smoking. I'd like to quit drinking about a fifth of whiskey a day and I'd like to eat sensibly."

Erickson asked him, *"Are you married?"* The policeman replied, *"No, I'm a bachelor. I do my own cooking, but there's a restaurant right around the corner where I often visit".*

Erickson said, *"So, there's a handy restaurant around the corner where you can dine. Where do you buy your cigarettes?"* He said he bought two cartons at a time. Erickson pointed out, *"In other words, you buy cigarettes not for today, but for the future. Now since you do most of your own cooking, where do you shop?"*

The policeman said, *"Fortunately, there's a little grocery store right around the corner. That's where I get my groceries and cigarettes."*

"Where do you get your liquor?" The policeman replied there was a liquor store right next door to the grocery.

"So you have a handy restaurant, grocery and liquor store near your house. You say you want to jog, but you can't. However, you CAN walk. All right, buy your cigarettes one pack at a time. Walk across town to buy your pack. That will get you in shape."

"As for groceries, don't go to the one by your place. Find another one at least a mile away. And buy just enough for one meal. That's three nice walks a day. As for the liquor, you can drink all you want to. Take your first drink at a bar at least a mile away. If you want a second drink, find another bar at least a mile away. If you want a third, find another bar a mile away."

The policeman looked at Milton Erickson angrily, cursed at him, and left. A month later, a new patient came by to see Erickson and told him this...*"A policeman referred me to you and said you were the only psychologist in town who knew what he was doing."*

The key to this story is that Erickson did not deprive this man of his desires. He did not say you cannot do this, or you must stop that. That is what well-meaning friends and family do, or what we impose on ourselves...and it never works.

Instead, Erickson tells the policeman what he CAN do. He can drink all he wants, smoke all he wants, and eat all he wants. But he must walk. He must change his patterns and routines.

What instructions could you give yourself right now to help transmute your bad habits into not so bad habits. How could you interrupt your patterns without depriving yourself of anything? Look at some areas of your life where you can make little shifts to yield huge results. Do not deprive yourself of what you view as a pleasure. Instead, interrupt your pattern. You might be surprised at the magnitude of the changes.

> *"How you do anything is how you do everything."*
> —Bruce D Schneider

11. DECISIONS

"The wisdom to make good decisions comes from good judgment.
Good judgment comes from experience.
Experience is often the result of making bad decisions."
—Universal Truth

People seem to get hung up on making decisions, which should be easy. You either want to do something or you don't. If you are not sure, it probably doesn't really matter anyway...like when you can't decide what to have for dinner.

"It doesn't matter which side of the fence you get off on sometimes. What matters
most is getting off. You cannot make progress without making decisions."
—Jim Rohn

For most of our decisions, does it really matter? Will the wrong choice really impact your life? Isn't making the wrong decision better than being stuck and un-empowered by not being able to decide?

"There is no more miserable human being
than the one in whom nothing is habitual but indecision."
—William James

Wisdom is not about making no mistakes...It is about learning to recover after we make them! Life would be so easy if we didn't make mistakes... but we do. In fact, we will continue to make errors for as long as we live. Now, does that make us unwise? Of course it doesn't... it makes us human!

As you already know, we can not foresee all things in life. We cannot plan everything out with certainty because there are too many variables and things to consider.

"Life is what happens when you're busy making other plans."
—John Lennon

So, accept that you will beget a few false moves as you live your life. Accept that you will not get everything right. Instead, resolve now to learn to cope with your errors. Determine to recover from them and mold things back together.

> *"Experience is not what happens to a man;*
> *it is what a man does with what happens to him."*
> —Aldous Huxley

For most decisions, there is an easy way to always know what to do… DO WHAT YOU WANT…as long as you consider the impact on yourself, other people, and the planet. Simple as that.

> *"In any moment of decision… the best thing you can do is the right thing.*
> *The second best thing you can do is the wrong thing.*
> *The worst thing you can do is nothing."*
> —Teddy Roosevelt

When people say they don't know…they really do know…they just do not like the intuitive guidance they are getting. When a client tells me they don't know, I ask "if you did know, what would it be"? or "What would it feel like if you did know"? Asking the right question reveals the answer.

For important choices, consider the type of decision you are trying to make, whether you are acting on a whim, a fantasy, a want, a should, or a need. Decide the consequences by running a movie in your head about the long term effects of this decision. Give your mind the gift of pause, and if it is a really important determination, wait a day or two after your decision to allow intuition to get into the picture. Take the decision from your head to your heart, to see if they are in harmony. Then ask yourself what values you are honoring with your decision versus any values you are violating.

If you end up on the wrong path, choose how you want to respond. After reading this book, that choice should be easy, as you will know to ask yourself the right questions. Ask questions that will move you forward.

Remember, all your decisions do not have to be perfect, but they should be satisfactory and sufficient to meet the needs of the particular situation. Stop having the compulsion to make perfect decisions. Just by doing that, you can lower your stress and be more at peace with the process of life. That's what you really want, isn't it?

"Every decision you make stems from what you think you are,
and represents the value that you put upon yourself."
—A Course in Miracles

Buddha believed that desire is the root of all suffering. I think what Buddha meant is the following: When you feel you need something to happen a certain way, or that your happiness is actually dependent on getting what you want... that is the root of all suffering.

Before we get to the final chapter, please let me emphasize that being intellectually aware of everything in this book is not enough. This information will have no impact on you unless you DECIDE to put forth the effort to make the changes you desire. If you think that by simply reading a book your life will change, then you are doing the same thing as believing that you can just pop a magic pill and it will fix everything. Nothing will change until you make the DECISION to change. The good news is... making that decision will be fun and rewarding.

"Success is the sum of small efforts, repeated day in and day out."
—Robert Collier

12. A GIFT FOR YOU

Earl Nightingale told a story many years ago called "Acres of Diamonds". He recounted a farmer who heard about acres of diamonds in the fields of Africa, sold his farm, and travelled to Africa to find these diamonds. Many years later, he died sad and broke. In the meantime, the people who bought his farm were digging one day and struck oil. The moral of the story is…are you looking for your happiness and good fortune somewhere else, when you are already standing upon it?

You possess a wonderful gift that you may not be using. It is the present. Do you live in the present, with all of its bounty, or are you spending your time in the past and the future?

> *"It is only possible to live happily ever after on a day to day basis."*
> —Margaret Bonnano

In his book, The Power of Now, Eckhart Tolle illustrates that people use the past for their identity and the future for their salvation. Are you spending a lot of time in the past? Do you think about regrets, disappointments, failures, what "they" did to you? Do you realize that the past only exists as a recording in your head? Are you relinquishing all of your free will by being a product of the "bad things" that happened in your past? Are you free to make choices, or are those choices directed by the past? Wayne Dyer says *"The wake does not drive the boat".* What is driving you?

Do not spend another minute mourning yesterday's failures, sadness, defeats, heartaches, and misfortunes. Can you relive the mistakes of yesterday and correct them? Can you take back the evil that was said, the pain that was caused? No. Yesterday is gone, and is only good for opportunities to learn and grow, not for regrets. Only use the past for memories that make you happy.

> *"I use memories, but no longer allow memories to use me."*
> —Old Indian Saying

"I could tell you my adventures...beginning from this morning"
said Alice a little timidly, "but it's no use going back to
yesterday, because I was a different person then."
—Alice in Wonderland

Do you use the future for your salvation? Will things be better when some particular event unfolds? Are you waiting for that impending event before your pleasure can arrive? Choosing to use your thought process this way may result in a brief episode of satisfaction when that approaching milestone occurs, but then you will create another impending event on which to dictate your future contentment. Is this how you have been operating? Are you wishing your life away? Are you discarding now for the sake of maybe?

Well...that's better than using the future as a source of fear, anxiety and worry... and continually creating movies in your mind about horrible looming developments. What will I do when this happens? What if I lose my job? Fail that test? He or she stops loving me? The list goes on. Do you project yourself into imaginary future situations and create fear? There is no way to cope with this future calamity because it does not exist...you are making it up.

"We can easily manage if we will only take, each day,
the burden appointed to it. But the load will be too heavy for us
if we carry yesterday's burden over again today, and then add the
burden of the morrow before we are required to bear it."
—John Newton

I was explaining to a friend that I am very happy in the present and am so passionate about the process of life that I do not ever worry about the future. I know that, whatever happens, there will always be peace inside of me. Then she said, yea, but what if...and went on to paint some horrible misfortunes. I answered, okay, so what if I really was to meet with catastrophe...shouldn't I deal with that then, not now? Shouldn't I wait to jump off that bridge until I get to it? Why should I create suffering for myself in the present by imagining something that may not ever happen? Why should I bring the problems of tomorrow into today?

"Some of your hurts you have cured, And the sharpest
you still have survived, But what torments of grief you
endured From the evil which never arrived."
—Ralph Waldo Emerson

Do not allow tomorrow's tragedy to cast its shadow backwards and lessen today's joy. Stop torturing yourself over things that may not occur, problems that may never come to fruition.

Wow…with all of this moving between the past and the future, no wonder we are so tired…we are always travelling.

> *"The mind is like a drunken monkey,*
> *forever jumping around, never staying steady."*
> —Zen saying

There is a simple way to stop this health eroding dance…stay in the present moment. Do you have any problems right this second? Take a deep breath and look around, right now…in the present. Enjoy the beauty of life, in all its glory. Right now…not next year, not tomorrow, not yesterday, not 30 years ago… right now. You can always cope with the present but you cannot control the future, and guess what…you do not have to. The right answer, the right action, the right thing will be there when you need it…not before, not after.

> *"When you are here and now, sitting totally, not jumping ahead,*
> *the miracle has happened. To be in the moment is the miracle."*
> —Osho

> *"In the race to be better and best, lest we forget to just be."*
> —Unknown

> *"Greet the sunrise with cries of joy and gratitude. Think of all who*
> *greeted yesterday's sunrise who are no longer among the living. Why*
> *were you given this day when others, maybe more deserving, were not?*
> *Is it that they have accomplished whatever their purpose was, and yours*
> *is yet to be achieved? Each hour of today should be cherished. What*
> *dying man wouldn't trade all of his gold to take one more breath?"*
> —Og Mandino

Life coach Nick Kolesnikoff, who combines ancient wisdom with modern knowledge in his book "Your Turn, Empowering Yourself to Change", explains:

> *"Avoid overtaxing your intellect. Do not assign your intellect anything that*
> *it was not designed to do. For example, do not ask it to predict the future;*
> *it simply cannot remember going forward. As a good soldier, it will try*

to be responsible and will make stuff up… unfortunately, since it doesn't really know, it will generate fear and anxiety." He goes on to explain "Understand what you control. You control, to some extent, your thoughts, words, and actions. You do not control outcomes…they are organized beyond your pay grade. Select your thoughts, words, and actions as if they bring consequences, good and bad, but don't attach yourself to their outcomes."

In the book "Conversations with God; An Uncommon Dialogue", Neale Donald Walsch explains the be-do-have paradigm, and how most people have it reversed:

"Most people believe that if they 'have' a thing (more money, time, love, whatever) then they can finally 'do' a thing (write a book, take up a hobby, go on vacation, buy a home, undertake a relationship) which will allow them to 'be' a thing (happy, peaceful, content, or in love). In actuality, they are reversing the Be-Do-Have paradigm. In the Universe, it really is (as opposed to how you think it is), 'havingness' does not produce 'beingness', but the other way around. First, you 'be' the thing called 'happy', (or 'knowing', or 'wise', or 'compassionate', whatever) then you start doing things from this place of being… and soon you discover that what you are doing winds up bringing you the things you've always wanted to 'have'. The way to set this creative process in motion (and that's what it is, the process of creation) is to look at what you want to 'have', ask yourself what you think you would 'be' if you 'had that', and then go right straight to being. In this way, you reverse the way you've been using the Be-Do-Have paradigm…in actuality, set it right, and work with, rather than against, the power of the universe. Here is a short way of stating this principle: In life, you do not have to do anything…it's all a question of what you are being."
—Neale Donald Walsch

Live in the present. Do not be driven by the need to "become" somebody. You are somebody right now. You are unique…you are rare. There is no one else like you. There is value in all rarity, therefore, you are valuable. You have been given eyes to see and a brain to think. You are able to see every setback, crisis, disappointment, and discouragement as a gift, an opportunity, and perhaps even a manifestation that life loves you, by encouraging you to go beyond the routine that you currently perform.

There isn't always going to be time later to live your dreams and be happy. Some day we all will run out of time…and it could be suddenly and without any notice. There are no guarantees. There is only this day.

There is only the present. Decide NOW what will make your life happy and fulfilling. Now is the time to take the steps necessary to achieve that fulfillment.

Become a believer...a believer in yourself and the capacity inside of you to be happier than you ever thought yourself capable. Be your authentic self, as there is no one more qualified for that job. When you trust that everything is happening just the way it is supposed to, an inner joy and energy emerges behind all you do and attempt. You are not driven by greed or lack. You are not crippled by fear. You do not seek certainty where it cannot be found, and don't fear the uncertainty that life will present. You do not seek love, you give love… you are love.

*"The job of expressing love, wisdom, and abundance in a creative way is yours as long as you want it. You have seniority. **No one is better at being you than you are.** You have no rivals, no competition. The universe is forever unfolding uniquely through you. Every situation at work is an opportunity to explore your beliefs about prosperity and life and to make a personal statement about those beliefs. Because you're part of creation, you are valuable. You play a vital, far reaching role in the universe. You are needed. You got the Job. Congratulations!"*
—Kathleen Hawkins – Spirit Incorporated

Avoid the compulsion to suffer when people and situations do not live up to your expectations. There is no need to judge people and situations. Release the thought that other people or situations make you happy…it is only you that can choose happiness.

Of course there will always be disappointments, frustrations, setbacks and even failures.…….that is just part of life. But in those challenging times you can still have an inner sense of calmness and joy…an underlying knowledge that you can weather any storm… and come out on the other side not only okay… but wiser, stronger, and better off from the experience.

"Your journey has molded you for your greater good and it was exactly what it needed to be. Don't think that you've lost time. It took each and every situation that you have encountered to bring you to the now…and now is right on time".
—Asha Tyson

Always remember that your happiness is determined more by your core energy and your beliefs than by any external event or other person. Success may cause a feeling of exhilaration, and tragedy or failure may result in a period of depression, but sooner or later your level of happiness will always return to its baseline. So...what have you chosen as your status quo?

"Your success and happiness lies in you. Resolve to keep happy,
and your joy and you shall form an invincible host against difficulties."
—Helen Keller

You are not a victim of life, but a master of your fate...able to create an existence overflowing with happiness, peace and love. The secret to happiness is in your hands, a fact that you will never again fail to realize.

"You had the power all along, my dear."
—Glinda, the Good Witch (The Wizard of Oz)

You are complete and perfect, just the way you are. Feel the glow of the light inside you and let it shine. How can you not be happy? How can you not bask in the bliss of Your Emotional Fitness?

"The best day of your life is the one in which you decide your life is your own.
No apologies or excuses. No one to lean on, rely on, or blame.
The gift is yours-an amazing journey-and you
alone are responsible for the quality of it.
This is the day your life really begins."
—Bob Moarwad

AFTERWORD - MY QUEST FOR EMOTIONAL FITNESS

As a result of difficulties throughout my childhood, I had low self esteem for a good portion of my life. This culminated in me being harsh with my words, so no one could take advantage of me. I now realize that unconsciously I was afraid that someone would. My core energy was that of anger.

In the 1980's I moved to Los Angeles to pursue the desire to become a movie star. After landing the role of "paramedic number two" on the soap opera "Days of Our Lives", I realized show business was not my passion. It was during this period in my life that I was first exposed to the motivational teachings of trainers such as Zig Ziglar, Brian Tracy, Tony Robbins and many others, and the motivational messages led me to a career in sales. After selling various mundane products, I entered the world of physical fitness. My first fitness job was at Beverly Hills Health and Fitness, as their sales manager. I was not drawn to the Los Angeles culture and longed for the more "laid back" attitude of San Diego. Sixteen months later, I saw a gym called Bodyworks advertised for sale in San Diego and I forged forward.

Throughout this book you have learned about the questions we ask ourselves and how they determine our destiny, and the question I asked myself was "How can I make this happen?" Although I was far from having a healthy level of emotional fitness, I did occasionally ask myself the right questions. In the chapter *Your Energy*, we discussed the existence of positives as well as negatives at all energy levels, and how anger energy can sometimes assist you with individual accomplishments. Sheer determination and hard work can also lead to success, but there are other, more effective ways to achieve your desired outcome.

When I first started managing Bodyworks, my sales style and way of dealing with vendors was overly aggressive, due to the unconscious programming from my childhood. I had difficulty letting my guard down, even for a minute, because fear of being victimized can result in anger energy as a means of protection from perceived threats. Some people cycle back and forth between victim and anger energy, but I remained in anger energy, determined not to ever be a victim. I owned Bodyworks until 1996, making my employees and members crazy with my manic, stressed out, and aggressive micro-managing style. My wife at the time was very tolerant, but my behavior necessitated the development of a code word to let her know that it was not safe to approach me, lest she be offended by my intense and negative energy.

In 1995 I heard about a gym in La Jolla called Club La Jolla, which was about to close down. Again, by asking myself the right questions, I was able to buy the gym, and remained there for the next 15 years. During these 15 years I was still an angry person, and would occasionally fly off the handle at the slightest provocation. In the chapter *How You Are Wired*, we discussed how people are influenced by past difficulties and, in an unconscious attempt to keep themselves safe, react to the slightest provocation as if hungry lions are jumping out at them. That was certainly the case with me. I referred to myself as a "stress monster." My adrenals were out of whack, and I was a basket of anxiety.

I mentored many people throughout this period, and would always say *"we all teach what we most need to learn"* as that was the case with me. As I mentored personal trainers, salespeople, receptionists, and others, I made them crazy with my manic style. On one hand, I was teaching them very important things about how to be successful in the world, and on the other hand I was demonstrating the opposite behavior. I couldn't see how others experienced me because I was controlled by unconscious programming, and even though I understood all the information about motivation and personal growth on a conscious level, I was still angry, frustrated, and not at peace with the process of life.

> *"You can read books, go to seminars, and learn all you want…*
> *but eventually you need to take a good look in the mirror."*
> —Jeff Carelli

After being at Club La Jolla for 15 years, I was ready for a change and merged with a competitor. The following year, I decided to get back into the fitness business, and was trying to purchase a gym that was failing. I mentioned to a friend, Duffy Doherty, that if I didn't close a certain deal, "I'd be devastated." He looked at me and said, "Wow, you are really out of balance. You should read *The Power of Now*, by Eckhart Tolle". Half way through the second reading, I felt a big weight lift off of my shoulders. It was the first time I had any idea how to stop the incessant chatter in my mind. You know the chatter I mean, obsessing about the past and worrying about the future, and trying to understand why things happen as they do. I started reading every book I could get my hands on that had anything to do with Personal Growth, Psychology, and Spiritual Psychology. I would sit in bookstores for hours finding books that resonated with me. Then I would sit for hours at coffee shops, on park benches, and at home reading.

A good friend, Mark Meyer, introduced me to life coach Cory Quigley, and suggested that I read her Ph.D. dissertation on Holistic Life Coaching. After reading the dissertation, called Generation Now, I knew that I wanted to be a life coach. In the past, while mentoring in health clubs and consulting to various businesses, I had unconsciously tried to make people believe that I was the smartest guy in the room. With life coaching, I learned that you can empower people to move from where they are to where they want to be, and in the process help them to realize that THEY are the smartest person in the room.

I spent several weeks researching Life Coaching Schools. There are hundreds, but only about 25 that are certified by the International Coach Federation (ICF). After all of my research, I enrolled in The Institute for Professional Excellence in Coaching (IPEC) for a 30 hour weekend class. Thanks to Keith Miller, the instructor, and the dynamic material provided by IPEC, I learned so much, mostly about myself, but also about how people operate. I immediately enrolled in their complete program for Life Coach training and certification.

I went on to take courses in Core Transformation, Hypnosis, and continued my study of Neural Linguistic Programming (NLP). After my NLP certification, I studied Metaphors of Movement, which is the exploration of the verbalization of non-verbal communications and behaviors. Simply put, sometimes the solution to our problems is to have a better understanding of the way we "construct" our problems in our mind.

Throughout my quest for emotional fitness, I experienced profound changes in my reality. My view of the world had changed and my relationships improved. I had less conflict in my life as I learned that conflict is never about right and wrong, but rather about stressful emotions emanating from a chaotic state of awareness. I no longer felt a need to be right, as I learned that the need to be right was simply allowing ego and insecurities to creep in and ruin an otherwise peaceful encounter. I finally understood that I could choose peace, happiness, and contentment as a way of being in the world.

Do I still get negative thoughts? Yes...but now I appreciate all of my emotions and understand that they are a call to action, letting me know something is amiss inside of me. They last long enough to signal that some kind of change is needed, and I handle them when they are small, as opposed to waiting until I am in crisis. For example, instead of letting things escalate until I am infuriated, I will make the change when I begin to get annoyed.

Do I believe I have attained emotional fitness? Certainly not...but I am closer to that place than I have ever been before. I do not know if it is possible to always be in a state of emotional fitness, but heading in that direction is a wonderful path to experience.

My "Next Chapter":

Throughout my quest for emotional fitness, I remained a true believer in the value of physical fitness. I believe that when you are fit both emotionally and physically, the rest of life seems to fall into place. Physical fitness is a relative term, as we will each have different definitions of what it means to be physically fit. A person with a debilitating condition will have a different definition than an Olympic athlete. Emotional fitness is so much easier to quantify. Are you happy? Fulfilled? Are you at peace with the process of life? Do you realize that pain is inevitable but suffering is optional?

Postscript on the fitness club deal...several months after I was unable to buy the club, the operator was evicted, the vacant space became available, and I was approached by a realtor to start a gym from scratch. Initially, I was intimidated as this was much bigger than anything I had ever done. However, I continued my Life Coach training and learned more about conditioned beliefs, the rules we unconsciously run our lives by, and the importance of the questions we ask ourselves. Instead of thinking that taking on a vacant 23,000 square foot space and starting a health club from scratch when I had very little money and had never created a new gym before was impossible, I asked myself "How can I make this happen"?

"Who says it can't be done? And what great accomplishments does he have to his credit to allow him to use the word 'impossible' so freely?"
—Napoleon Hill

The challenges seemed insurmountable, and although well meaning friends suggested I move on as this opportunity was well beyond my reach, I believed that this particular building and location was an absolutely perfect and rare opportunity. You've learned throughout this book to not let other people's limiting beliefs and opinions become your reality.

"Whatever you believe, you get to be right about and experience."
—IPEC Foundation Principal

Next came many months of delays, obstacles, setbacks and challenges. I truly believe that if I had not allowed the ideas contained within the pages of this book into not just my mind but also my heart, I would not have had the ability to bring my dream to a successful finish.

Instead, armed with the right core energy, I turned every setback into an advantage. Every time something went wrong, I asked myself "How can this work to my benefit?" As you know, our brains will always answer the questions that we ask ourselves (chapter 2.2). Every time a disagreement occurred, I would envision things from the other person's point of view, as well as my own (chapter 4 and chapter 6.1). Before going into a negotiation, I would center myself with the method you learned in chapter 2.4, where I would breathe in the white light of confidence, ease, insight, or whatever feeling I thought would be of benefit to myself and everyone involved.

Whenever I heard that voice in my head (chapter 2.7) telling me that this was too big...beyond my reach...I would question whose voice it was, my current voice of reason, or just some scary noises out of my past. Then I would just turn down the volume, way down, giving no energy to the voice and allowing it to fade away...until it became a feeling I used to know (chapter 2.1).

As I sit here putting the finishing touches on this chapter, I am in my fourth year of operation, having signed the lease, taken possession of the premises and operated successfully now for several years.

When I began the journey that started when I took possession of the club space, I believed that I should remain at energy level 5 (chapter 2.2). At energy level 5, everything is seen as an opportunity and the core thought is on reconciling differences rather than focusing on ways to change them. It is a true win–win mentality. Level 5 served me well. During construction, there were many challenges, as I did this project without the appropriate financing. One major challenge I encountered during this period was when the club was broken into and vandalized. My response was to simply ask myself how this event could work to my benefit. Ultimately, I understood that life is very simple…things happen, and we get to choose how to interact with the reality of the situation (chapter 3.2). The whole event ended up being of benefit to the big picture. The Your Energy chapter also stated that there are no good or bad energy levels, only appropriate levels of energy, but I had forgotten that part. I had an employee who was becoming a problem. I remained at level 5 when it was not the appropriate level. Lesson learned. There are no good or bad energy levels, only appropriate energy levels.

When challenges arose and the voice in my head (chapter 2.7) asked *"how can I make this situation fulfill my needs?"* I would become present and instead ask *"how do I respond to the needs of this situation?"* In doing so, I became one with the situation and allowed the solution to arise from the situation itself (chapter 1.2). Once the solution presented itself, I was careful to not let ego get involved, knowing that taking credit for the accomplishment would be the end of the creativity that arises from inner spaciousness and non resistance.

The only thing that mattered was happiness (See chapter 4.8, "How To Be Happy"). Too many people think that happiness, like success, is something you become. In reality it is something to be, without limiting conditions (as explained in chapter 4.8). During challenging times, I simply surrendered to "what is." Consequently, there were never any problems, only events that I needed to deal with. All I ever really had to deal with were my own fears or desires (chapter 2.7).

Decisions (chapter 9) were easy, as our mantra is "If it's good for the staff, good for the members, and good for the club, we can do it". Understanding that success is never anything other than a successful present moment, we are free from fear of failure (chapter 6.1). When we eliminate pressure to produce results at any cost, and instead follow our inner wisdom and trust in the process of life, events often unfold better than we could have ever imagined (chapter 1.2 and chapter 4.2)

The best part is that the club has exceeded the vision. It was born of a belief that a health club should be a place where you not only exercise your body, but you also receive an emotionally uplifting experience. My vision has always been to share an experience that enhances the physical, emotional, and spiritual well being of everyone involved.

Everything fell into place for me to move forward with effortless ease. If you ask me for the key to achieving this goal, I would say it is because I trusted in the principles contained within this book, and that I put them into action.

> *"You are perfect. You are complete.*
> *Your inner voice always knows what to do,*
> *but it is a quiet voice.*
> *You can only hear the whisperings of your inner voice -*
> *your inner compass - when you turn down the volume*
> *of your fears, your regrets, your resentments,*
> *and the fear-based advice*
> *your neighbors are so willing to give you."*
> —Jonathan Lockwood Huie

Remember, it is never a matter of what you are doing…it is always a matter of what you are being. To achieve inner peace, contentment, and success is my wish for you.

"Be committed to trusting in the process of life…"

ACKNOWLEDGEMENTS

My biggest thank you goes to my sister Shelley, for the countless hours she spent helping me with the re-write and editing of both this book and the original book. Without her help, we would not be here together, with you as the reader and me as the author.

Thank you to Leslie Gladstone for all of your help with editing and the final re write.

Thank you to my sister Debbie, just for being you.

Thank you to my daughter Jessica and my daughterish type person Selena… for being awesome in all the ways that matter.

Thank you to the entire staff at Point Loma Sports Club for helping to make my vision of the most awesome Fitness Club in creation a reality.

Thank you to everyone who read the first version of Your Emotional Fitness, and especially those that gave me feedback on how much it helped your emotional fitness.

Thank you to all of the Authors and Masters that contributed to my knowledge, which gave me the ability to write this book. As I stated in chapter 1.2, this book is a compilation of over 25 years of learning. Throughout the book, I have tried to give credit where I could, realizing that it is not always possible, as the information that is learned will sometimes become inseparable from the student. It can be difficult to know where a memory of something learned leaves off and a creative thought begins. My major influences have been Michael Singer, Deepak Chopra, Eckhart Tolle, and Lao Tzu.

> "The teacher who is indeed wise does not bid you to enter the house of his wisdom, but rather leads you to the threshold of your own mind."
> —Kahlil Gibran

Some of the books and authors that I would like to credit with their contributions to my growth, and therefore their contributions to this book are: The Untethered Soul- Michael Singer, A New Earth- Eckhart Tolle,

The Power of Now-Eckhart Tolle, The Search for Truth- Michael Singer, Three Essays on Universal law- Michael Singer, The Seven Spiritual Laws of Success- Deepak Chopra, The Fifth Agreement-Don Miguel Ruiz, The Biology of Belief- Bruce Lipton, Energy Leadership- Bruce D. Schneider, Change Your Thoughts; Change Your Life- Wayne Dyer, The Surrender Experiment,- Michael Singer, Stillness Speaks-Eckhart Tolle, Reinventing the Body, Resurrecting the Soul-Deepak Chopra, The Mastery of love-Don Miguel Ruiz, The Four Agreements- Don Miguel Ruiz, The Inside Out Revolution- Michael Neill, Supercoach- Michael Neill, The Seat of the Soul- Gary Zukaw, The Heart of the Soul- Gary Zukaw, You Can Heal Your Life- Louise Hay, Your Turn...Empowering Yourself to Change- Nick Kolesnikoff, Think and Grow Rich-Napoleon Hill, The Greatest Salesman in the World-Og Mandino, Awaken the Giant Within- Anthony Robbins, Unlimited Power- Anthony Robbins, Core Transformation- Connirae & Tamara Andreas, NLP The New Technology of Achievement- Steve Andreas & Charles Faulkner, Laws of Success-Napoleon Hill, Emotional Wisdom- Mantak Chia and Dena Saxer, Top Performance-Zig Ziglar, Outliers- Malcolm Gladwell, What the Bleep do we Know-William Arntz, Betsy Chasse, Mark Vicente, Advanced Energy Anatomy- Carolyn Myss, The Art of Happiness- Dalai Lama & Howard C. Cutler, The Wisdom of No Escape- Pema Chodron, Leadership Potentials Training- IPEC, Coach Training Manuals 1...2...3- IPEC, The Five Love Languages- Dr. Gary Chapman, Illusions- Richard Bach, Conversations with God- Neale Donald Walsch, Mans Search for Meaning- Victor Frankl, Deep Truth- Greg Braden, Anatomy of an Illness- Norman Cousins, Tao te Ching- Lao Tzu, Flow: The Psychology of Optimal Performance- Mihaly Csikszentmihalyi, Psycho Cybernetics- Dr. Maxwell Maltz, The Prophet-Kahlil Gibran SEMINARS & WORKSHOPS: Core Transformation-Tamara Andreas, Metaphors of Movement- Andrew Austin, IPEC Coach Training-Keith Miller, Energy Leadership- Dr. Bruce Schneider, NLP Practitioner Training- Dr. Mathew James, Hypnosis Training- Nickolas Rave, Unleash the Power Within- Tony Robbins, The Psychology of Achievement- Brian Tracy.

And finally, many thanks to you, the reader of this book, for allowing me the privilege and honor of helping you to realize your emotional fitness. If this book inspired you, please read it again, and then pass it on to someone that you believe it will inspire.

ABOUT THE AUTHOR

Gary Rubin is a life coach, business consultant, entrepreneur, and health club owner/operator in San Diego California. He has spent over 25 years committed to enhancing his own personal growth by researching, studying, and training in the fields of personal growth, psychology, and spiritual psychology. He has attained his certifications as a Professional Life Coach, Practitioner of Neuro Linguistic Programming, and Master Practitioner of the Energy Leadership Index. As a business coach and consultant, he has successfully mentored and coached business owners, managers, and employees; resulting in greater productivity and profitability. As a life coach, he has worked with individuals, couples, and families, helping them to achieve personal growth, enhanced life satisfaction, conflict resolution, and emotional fitness. Gary is now involved in managing his health club, *Point Loma Sports Club*, (www.plsportsclub.com) in San Diego California. He has occasional availability for personal and business coaching, consulting, and speaking engagements. Please contact him at www.YourEmotionalFitness.com

SOME FINAL THOUGHTS FOR YOU...

"If the only prayer you said in your whole life was
Thank You, that would suffice."
—Meister Eckhart

"Don't require the Universe to move more rapidly than it is.
It is actually working perfectly, and it will prove that to you if
you will give it a chance. Really. Trust me on this."
—Neale Donald Walsch

"When you learn what the world is, how it works,
You automatically start getting miracles... what others call miracles"
—Richard Bach

"Everything had to unfold exactly as it did for 13.8 billion years for the
moment to be how it is. So honor and respect your right to experience it."
—Michael Singer

"You can argue 20 different point of view in intellectual matters
But with mysteries of spirit and love, it is best to be bewildered
In an ocean with no edge, what good are swimming skills"
—Rumi

"When your mind is your servant and not your master,
you will have a fullness of spirit which overflows,
along with a lifestyle of more than adequate material provisions."
—Gary Rubin